Harry Cole

Policeman's Progress

FONTANA/Collins

First published in Great Britain
in 1980 by Fontana Paperbacks,
8 Grafton Street, London W1X 3LA
Ninth impression June 1988

Copyright © Harry Cole 1980

Printed and bound in Great Britain by
William Collins Sons & Co. Ltd, Glasgow

The views expressed in this book are the author's own
and do not necessarily reflect the official views of
the Metropolitan Police

Policeman's Progress

Harry Cole was born and brought up in Bermondsey, south London. He left school when he was fourteen, during the war, and became a cricket-bat maker, soldier, stonemason and, in 1952, a policeman. For thirty years, until his retirement in 1983, he served at the same police station in London.

He is a qualified FA coach (he has run numerous junior football teams), a referee and a keen cricketer. For many years he had a regular column in the *Warren*, the police magazine. His other books are *Policeman's Lot*, *Policeman's Patch*, *Policeman's Patrol*, *Policeman's Prelude* and *Policeman's Story*, his two-volume autobiography, *Policeman's Gazette* and *The Blue Apprentices*, a novel.

In 1978 Harry Cole was awarded the British Empire Medal for voluntary work. Since leaving the force, in addition to writing he has taken up after-dinner speaking.

To Tony Parker,
for his
encouragement

Contents

1. Should I Stay?

'The weather for the capital area will be extremely hot, ~~with~~ temperatures reaching the low nineties by the early ~~afternoon.~~' The mid-Atlantic drawl of the disc jockey ~~roused~~ my apathy as I slowly patrolled the baking Wharf Road pavement in Southwark. I turned to see the source of my annoyance. I was surprised to see young Glen Ervine sitting behind the wheel of a rusty, ten-year-old sports car. The radio was blaring and the engine snarled impatiently as the last of the pedestrians made their way over the crossing. Sitting beside Glen was Sandra Harrison. On seeing me Sandra's face broke into a huge smile and she waved cheerily.

Glen was in his early twenties and I had known him since he was a kid. He was a small-time and very unsuccessful thief. There was also a warrant in existence for his arrest. He had not paid a fine for the third time of asking and the magistrate was showing some impatience. Glen had been 'seeing to' Sandra for some time now, and local rumour had it that she was four months pregnant. She was a nice kid really, quite pretty but not very bright. Roaring around the back streets of Southwark in a 'flashy' car would give her a degree of status among her friends out of all proportion to its worth. Sandra would love every minute of it and who could begrudge her? Life fairly soon would be smacking her right between the eyes.

I began to move towards the car, then changed my mind. Glen could be picked up at any time and Sandra

looked really happy. It would be a pity to spoil her pleasure. In any case, it was just too hot to go around nicking people. Sandra looked up at me. Concern was beginning to show in her face.

'Everything all right, Mr Cole?'

'Yes, just turn the radio down a bit, Sandra, please,' I replied.

'Sure. Ta-ta!' she called as Glen accelerated away in a cloud of blue, cancerous smoke.

I waved back in acknowledgement. The simple movement exhausted me.

At no time during our conversation did Glen look up. Almost as an afterthought I called the station on my personal radio to check the car's registration number. The call came back in seconds from the computer operator. 'Red MGB stolen from Peckham two days ago.' I momentarily closed my eyes. I'll kill that bloody Sandra.

A summer like this should only happen to a policeman early in his career. He can then spend the rest of his service reminiscing about it. To happen near the end of his service is hardly fair. If only I had experienced a summer like this twenty-five years ago when I joined the force! I could have gathered a group of recruits about me in the canteen and said things like, 'Don't tell me you're hot? That's the trouble with the youngsters of today, no stamina. Now I can remember a summer twenty years ago . . .'

Policemen, as a breed, suffer more than most from extremes of weather because they also have to contend with the uniform designers. For example, on this particular day I was wearing a heavy nylon tunic-shirt that buttoned up to the neck. Those of us who had to wear the things reckoned the designer had been an inmate of Dartmoor falsely imprisoned for murder. He was exacting a dreadful revenge. It was 9.45 a.m. and my back was streaming like Niagara.

I was on my way down to 32 Bronte House, a third-floor tenement flat. A telephone call had been received at the Wharf Road station, saying that Miss Elsie Morton of that address had not been seen for some weeks and neighbours feared that something had happened to her.

Elsie was no stranger to me. I had called on her for exactly the same reason on three previous occasions and each time she had given me a verbal hiding. She was a seventy-year-old recluse who rarely ventured outside her front door. Actually her 'front door' was half of the problem. Most of the flats in Bronte House were situated on long narrow balconies, eight to a floor. Each flat had a bathroom window on the left side of the door and a toilet window on the right side. If entry had to be gained, either the bathroom or lavatory window could easily be forced. However, each floor level also had just one flat with an entrance on the staircase. This consisted of a door which opened into an internal passage which turned immediately left for a distance of some six yards before emerging into a living-room. (The architect was on par with our shirt designers.) If Elsie did not want to answer the door – and in my experience she never did – it was the devil's own job to persuade her.

I was not in a good temper, Sandra had seen to that. Elsie would take ages to answer the door, if in fact she ever did. The torrent of abuse she would pour on me would have been bearable on a normal day but today was just too bloody hot. I wearily climbed the stairs to a third floor and I was greeted by three of her neighbours. On each previous occasion that I had called, I had been met by the same three women. They were amazing. Facially they did not look alike, also the hair of each was a different colour, but in every other contour they were identical. They were the same height, build and age (about fifty). Their hair had been back-combed and bird's-nested by

the same hairdresser. The dark green overall with 'Twentieth-Century Cleaners' emblazoned over their ample left breasts indicated that they were either office cleaners working for the same firm, or one of their husbands worked in the stores. They reminded me of a set of plump jugs.

'It's Elsie, Mr Cole,' said the first woman.

'What's the matter this time?' I replied somewhat irritably.

'Ain't seen her for nearly a month,' said another woman.

'Perhaps she's gone away,' I ventured optimistically but somewhat unconvincingly.

'No one would 'ave her, she smells!' said the first. I had to agree there. To say that Elsie 'smelled' was the understatement of the year. With Elsie it was not the smell that I objected to, it was the taste. It got down the back of my throat and lay there like a crust. I could smell it hours afterwards. With the temperature in the nineties the stench would be spiteful.

I peeped through Elsie's letter-box. The piece of sacking that hung down inside to keep out the winter draughts obscured any view. There was no bell or knocker, so I placed my back to the door and crashed my heel hard several times against the panelling. The noise reverberated throughout Bronte House. The pigeons scavenging in the yard fluttered up fussily for a few seconds but soon settled again. Passers-by in the street looked up; several of the remaining paint flakes fell to the ground but Elsie was obviously unmoved.

'Elsie!' I yelled. 'Come on, luv, open the door!'

There was no reply.

'Come on, Elsie, it's me, PC Cole, just let me see if you're okay.'

I kicked at the door once more. This time the pigeons

glanced up contemptuously.

'I fink she's 'ad it this time, Mr Cole,' said Ada, the first woman.

'She shouldn't be left on her own, in my opinion,' added Rennie, the second.

I looked expectantly at Maggie, woman number three, but she just shook her head. A heavy silence returned to the staircase.

I now had a problem. How to gain entrance to number thirty-two. There was no way through the door. It would have to be an outside window. I could ring the fire brigade but if Elsie discovered a fireman trying to get into her bedroom she would most probably push him clean off his ladder. At least she *knew* me. Perhaps I will ring the brigade and ask to climb the ladder myself. Rennie broke into my dilemma.

'The painters are working in the flats opposite,' she said.

'So?' I queried.

'I just thought you may be able to borrow a ladder.'

Of course! Why is it that I cannot think quickly when it gets hot? I would have made a rotten Arab.

Ten minutes later I had spoken to the foreman painter and he and his lad soon had the ladder propped beneath Elsie's window sill.

'Be a bit careful getting in, guv',' said the foreman. 'We ly painted it last week.'

'How did you get into the flat?' I asked hopefully.

'We didn't, she wouldn't answer the door, so we inted it from outside.'

left my helmet with Rennie and began to climb the rungs. Ladders and I are not compatible and it was with some trepidation that I saw the ladder stopped six inches short of the sill. I intended to stand near the top and lift up the bottom half of the window, which was the old-

fashioned sash-cord type. My first job was to peep into the room. On reaching the window sill I could see that this was going to be no easy task. The frame may have been painted last week but the glass had not been cleaned for years. In addition the curtains were drawn. I could see no more from my ladder than I could through the letter-box. Elsie Morton, I thought, you are a cussed old cow!

There was only one thing left now. I had to break one of the panes of glass. Since the police had been issued with personal radios, I had ceased to carry a truncheon. The weight on my trousers had been just too much. I had once put up both my hands on a school crossing and almost lost my trousers. Something had to go. So I decided that it would be my truncheon. Right now I bitterly regretted that decision.

I reached down and took off my right shoe. After a surprising number of thumps, I eventually broke a small pane and inserted my hand to pull back the curtain. I looked down at Elsie's bed. Elsie stared straight back at me. At least I thought it was Elsie. The creature that I could see was shrivelled, black and covered with maggots. The stench flooded out of that broken window and so did the flies. I clambered quickly down the ladder, half-falling the last few steps.

'Wassamatter, mate? Is she all right?' said a female voice amongst the spectators.

I answered by calling the station on my radio.

'Could I have the divisional surgeon, please? Miss Morton is well dead.'

A hubbub ran around the crowd. I leaned against the ladder waiting for the reply that would reluctantly take me back into that dreadful room. My radio spluttered into life.

'The divisional surgeon will be with you in half an hour.'

There was nothing else for it, I would have to gain

access to that room to open the door for the doctor. Without his say-so, Elsie officially was not dead! I climbed slowly back up the ladder.

'Wouldn't have his job for a fortune,' I heard a by-stander remark.

'Why not?' answered another. 'They're trained for it, ain't they?'

'Trained for it!' Bloody fool! I was about as at home on this ladder as if it had been the north face of the Eiger.

I finally reached the sill and pulled at the bottom of the window. It would not budge. There was one unbroken coat of paint over the frame, sill and glass. I had visions of giving an extra tug, the window flying up and me flying down. I looked at the crowd below; they were obviously enjoying the same idea. There is nothing like a bit of gore to draw a crowd, and a copper breaking his neck could be class-one entertainment. I studied the window again. If I could not pull the bottom half up, perhaps I could pull the top half down. After a few minutes of banging and pulling, it began to move. Eventually I had a gap of about eighteen inches.

My plan had been to enter the room head-first, via the top of that window. I was going to reach down to the interior ledge, then quickly swing my legs round and regain my balance, just the instant before I hit the floor. The bed being immediately under the window caused me to change that scheme. The temperature may have been in the nineties but the thought of plunging head-first on to that corpse gave me the shivers. It was doubtful if Elsie Morton had shared a bed with a man during the whole of her seventy years alive. I did not wish to be responsible for that little adventure four weeks after she had died!

I stood with my left foot on the top rung and inserted my right leg through the gap at the top of the window. I

15

suddenly saw the tip of my right big toe peeping through my sock. In all the trauma I had forgotten to replace my shoe! I paused momentarily. I would look a complete idiot if I went down that ladder yet again – ''Ere, excuse me, has anyone seen my shoe?' – no, better to carry straight on and pretend that it is part of some grand overall police policy to enter all third-floor windows without a right shoe. I inserted my right leg deeper into the room. My left leg stretched to tip-toe. I bent my head into the opening and with my chin almost on my knee, my left foot relinquished its hold at the top of the ladder.

My shoeless right foot waved around searching for the inside sill, without success. My back was pressed hard against the top of the window frame. I was stuck tight. The position wasn't encouraging. I am middle-aged, frightened of heights, three floors up and sweating like a pig. I am besieged by flies, I couldn't go forward and I couldn't go back. The pressure on my groin was placing my manhood in great danger. I had on only one shoe and a hole in my sock! What the hell was I doing here? My hand searched for the transmitting button of my personal radio, when suddenly I was hit by the potential of the situation. If I called for assistance, my colleagues would have no choice but to call the fire brigade (who incidentally I now wished I had called in the first place) and I most certainly would never be allowed to forget this saga. Each time I set foot in the station for the next few months I would be ribbed unmercifully. ''Ullo, Romeo! Couldn't you git up the ladder then?' I decided to risk all on one last push.

I lurched forward and as I plunged into the room, I instantly felt a burning sensation along the curve of my spine. I knew that once I began to move I would need to keep going, otherwise I would finish up alongside, or on top of Elsie. I was vaguely aware of my shoeless foot landing on something soft. Whether it was the bedding or

the corpse I was not sure. I did not stay long enough to find out. I ricocheted across the room and crashed against the wardrobe. Flies rose in one huge mass, they were everywhere. The sweat that streamed down my face drew them like jam. The pain in my testicles felt as though a camel-trader had just given me a vasectomy with two bricks. I regained my balance and took stock. I had received no more than a torn shirt, a grazing along my back and a dull ache in my 'rude' bits. I had visions of a broken leg and a rupture, and lying on that bed with Elsie whilst waiting for assistance. All in all, I had been extremely lucky.

The body lay on a single bed with one arm raised above its head, as if warding off some evil spirit. It was clad in only a filthy vest, and the bedding consisted of tattered remnants, mainly old coats and blankets. The room was furnished with just a wooden chair alongside the bed, a small dresssing table with a broken mirror, and of course the wardrobe that I had already met. The bare lino seemed covered with little black stains and there was a chipped enamel chamber-pot underneath the bed. Dust and insect life abounded. Oh how I wished I had two shoes!

I made my way quickly to the door, intending to let some air into the flat. I also needed to find out from neighbours if Elsie had any next-of-kin. A crunching under my feet caused me to look down and I realized that the 'little black stains' were in fact little black beetles. I hopped on one foot to the passage, which was comparatively clean, and eventually I unbolted the door. The first person I saw was Rennie.

'D'you want yer shoe, Mr Cole?' she said, stretching out her hand.

I resisted the temptation to give her a big kiss and simply said: 'Thanks, Rennie. Do you know if she had any relatives?'

'The only person who may be able to help you is old Nelly Addison. She lives at number five on the ground floor. They used to be friends at one time. Can we see Elsie, Mr Cole?' said Rennie, who had now been joined by Ada and Maggie.

'Well you can, but I wouldn't advise it. It's pretty grim in there. Although I would appreciate it if you could keep an eye on the place, while I have a word with Nelly Addison,' I answered.

'Leave it to us, mate,' said Ada, and the three of them disappeared into the dingy passageway.

I ran down the stairs to the ground floor. The door of number five was open and a stout old lady with a stick stood in the entrance.

'Hullo, luv,' I greeted, 'are you Nelly Addison?'

'Yes, come in, sir,' she replied and turning, slowly hobbled along the passage and into the living-room. I followed. I could not understand how Nelly and Elsie used to be friends, they appeared to be worlds apart. The flat was absolutely spotless. The leaves of the rubber-plant that stood by the door positively gleamed.

'Elsie's dead, is she, sir?' murmured the old lady.

''Fraid so, luv. Do you know if she had any relatives?'

'Yes, she had a niece.'

'Would you know her name and address?'

'Well I don't know her Christian name but her surname is Evans and she lived somewhere in Wales,' she said hopefully.

'Is that it!' I exclaimed somewhat incredulously.

'Yes, sir, except that Elsie had money, you know.'

'Where?'

'Dunno, sir, she was ever so cagey, but it will be in the flat somewhere,' said Nelly, shaking her head wisely.

This was the worst possible news to me. I was hoping that there would be a convenient next-of-kin to whom I

could hand over everything once the doctor had pronounced life extinct. In addition there was the money. If I did not find it, the neighbours would be convinced that I had pocketed it. The thought of searching those rooms caused my stomach to heave.

I returned to Elsie's flat. Standing in the doorway was Alf, the block caretaker. He was talking to a large, smartly dressed man, who was carrying an attaché case in his right hand and sporting a huge carnation in his left lapel. A doctor, if ever I saw one, but it was not our usual divisional surgeon, who was away on holiday.

'Morning, officer! What have we got?' he boomed.

'A recluse, sir; she looks like she has been dead for some time,' I volunteered.

'I see. What can you tell me about her?'

I gave him what little information I had.

'Let us take a look, shall we?' He was looking at me but talking to the world at large. He followed me down the passage. On reaching the bedroom door, I noticed he did not step into the room but he put his head round the door.

'Good God! What a mess! Yes, well, dead some weeks I'd say. Anything else I can do before I go?'

'Not unless you'd like to take her with you,' I said somewhat ruefully. He's the bloody doctor, in and out in a flash, collecting a nice fat fee, and I had got Elsie until I could get rid of her to someone. I was not thrilled.

'Oh well, cheerio, then,' he called. Some seconds later, his Volvo purred out of the yard. Even the pigeons looked impressed.

I pressed the transmitter button on my radio and called the station.

'Doctor certified life extinct. No relatives. Can you request the coroner's officer to send an undertaker please?'

'Stand by,' replied Bernadette, our communications officer.

As I stood waiting at the door of the flat I saw Rennie walking towards me with a glass of beer in her hand.

'Want a drink, luv?' she said.

'What an angel!' I exclaimed.

I was half-way through drinking it when my radio spluttered. Bernadette's voice came over clearly but somewhat apologetically.

'The coroner's officer is a bit busy. He'll arrange for the undertaker to be with you in about a couple of hours. He's got some sort of delay.'

I nearly drowned in my beer.

'He'll have an even longer one if he is not here inside thirty minutes,' I snapped back. 'She's decomposing and I'm melting. The flat stinks and it's running alive. I cannot find the keys and once the door is shut the only way in is forty feet up a ladder. He can either get here in half an hour or get in the same way I did. But one thing is for sure; I'm not stopping here for another two hours!'

I was not sure how much of that dialogue breached the official RT procedure on 'Use of personal radios', but I was beyond caring. Actually I was quite ashamed of my reaction and was instantly sorry for poor Bernadette. Five minutes later she called back.

'Undertaker will be with you in twenty minutes.'

I walked back on to the balcony and finished my beer in peace.

Three floors below, the caretaker had resumed sweeping the yard. It had just occurred to me that to search that flat on my own would make me as vulnerable as a one-legged spider. Supposing the money was not found? I knew Alf slightly and called for him to come up. I explained the situation and he readily agreed to help.

The flat consisted of a kitchen, living-room, bedroom, bathroom and toilet. It was sparsely furnished and the

only food we found was a packet of biscuits. Cupboard after cupboard was empty. However there were three large bundles of good quality clean clothing. These were in their original wrappings and had been provided by some voluntary organization but never used.

'There ain't no money in this flat, guv'. We've searched just about everywhere,' said Alf.

'We have, with the exception of the bed, Alf. How do you feel about searching the old girl herself?'

Alf thrust his hand deep into his overall pockets and, by way of a reply, pulled out a pair of heavy rubber gloves. He inserted his hands into the bedding and ran his hands quickly up and down the length of the bed.

'Nothing,' he said.

'How about underneath her?' I countered.

Alf grimaced. He grabbed the blackened corpse by the hair and pulled it firmly up into a sitting position. Another great cloud of angry flies rose. There it was! A large leather wallet covered with several elastic bands and lying just under the base of Elsie's spine.

Alf let the body fall back. There was a sickening squelch and we both hastened out of the bedroom. Alf scattered the contents of the wallet on to the bare wooden kitchen table and gave a low whistle. In the main it consisted of five and ten pound notes. We checked and double-checked. £721! A pound of biscuits and seven hundred and twenty-one quid!

Oh you bloody fool, Elsie.

'Anyone at home?' I looked up to see Sid Crouch, the Wharf Road undertaker, walking down the passage. He was followed by a cheerful-looking lad of about twenty, who was, I presumed, his new assistant.

''Ullo, struck lucky then?' said the smiling youth, beaming at the money.

'Just a minute, Alf,' I said quickly. 'Sign the amount in

my pocket-book. We both need to be protected.' Alf obliged.

'Where's the body, officer?' said the undertaker.

I placed the wallet in my trouser pocket and led them into the bedroom. On seeing the remains of Elsie the smiling assistant chirupped:

'Oh dear! She don't look well at all.'

I stared at the youth in total disbelief. He had only been in my life one minute and already I hated him. Sid glared at him over the top of his spectacles.

'Go and get the "shell", Stevie,' he snapped.

The lad reddened visibly and quickly left the room.

'He's all right really,' said Sid somewhat apologetically, 'just a little immature.'

'As an undertaker, I reckon he'd make a bleedin' good bingo-caller,' muttered Alf almost to himself.

The assistant returned in a few minutes, with a slim light-weight coffin which appeared to be made of leather. He placed it alongside the bed.

'Do you want a hand?' I offered with all the insincerity at my disposal.

'No thanks, she's almost a midget,' replied Sid.

He was right about that. I doubt if Elsie was much more than four feet ten inches in height. Both Sid and his apprentice pulled on a pair of stout gloves and rolled the body from that dreadful bed and into the shell. The flies instantly rose again and, being deprived of their haven, buzzed angrily around the room. I noticed Elsie's hand was still raised above her head. Sid placed the lid on the shell and secured it around the centre with a broad leather strap. The tightening caused each end of the lid to lift slightly and I could see the flies were still busy to-ing and fro-ing. Sid bade us farewell and he and Stevie hoisted up the box on to their shoulders. They filed down the passageway in that slow, deliberate way that undertakers have. I believe they even run for buses with the same economy of movement. However, when they reached the door, the angle was too great to turn with the shell in its horizontal position.

'Stand her up!' called Sid. As the coffin was tilted on to its end, there was a scraping noise as Elsie slid down to the bottom of the box.

Several of the neighbours had waited on the balcony to pay their last respects. Ada, Rennie and Maggie were well to the fore and each of them carried their handkerchiefs in their hands. On leaving the door, Sid and Stevie again hoisted the shell on to their shoulders and slowly, and with great professional dignity, moved towards the stairs. The image was tarnished by the constant stream of flies buzzing in and out from under the partially raised lid.

Stevie began to descend the stairs and Sid was the regulation three paces behind him. I could see that Sid was having trouble finding the first step. Stevie, being somewhat inexperienced, did not seem to realize Sid's difficulty and the angle of the coffin became very acute. Suddenly there was the scraping noise again as Elsie rushed once more to the head of the box and her hand appeared from under the lid, as if waving a last farewell.

Alf suddenly appeared at my side.

'I've found the keys, guv', they were in the bed as well,' he said.

I was delighted. I could now close the door and leave the council to clean up. I thanked everyone for their assistance and made my way back to the station.

I left the precincts of Bronte House with no little relief. I had about three-quarters of a mile to walk back to the 'nick'. I was planning how to cover most of the route in the maximum amount of shade. Suddenly I was aware of a little old lady heading straight towards me.

I groaned inwardly. If I had a choice of people that I did not wish to meet at that particular moment then Miss Ethel Robinson, aged about seventy-two years, would be extremely high on that list. Ethel was a compulsive complainer. There was not a subject she had not complained about over the years. If it moved; stood still; flew; played football; smoked; rolled; made a sound; or wobbled; Ethel would be on to it in a flash.

She was not on the telephone at home, yet she would venture out on the coldest nights as many as three or four times, just to find a phone box and make her '999' calls. Most of the station mobile units had developed an 'anti-Ethel' system over the years. On receiving the call, they would go like a bat out of hell to her home address. This was in an effort to race her back from the telephone kiosk. A quick knock on her front door, no answer and the station message pad could be marked up 'No reply'. The amazing thing was that Ethel never complained about this. She just seemed to accept it as part of the game that she played.

Ethel always prefaced every complaint with the words: 'I must tell you this.' The trouble was that Ethel could never make any complaint in under twenty minutes, and usually it took a great deal longer. The mid-day temperature was still in the nineties. The thought of standing still in that heat listening to Ethel for the next half-hour appalled me.

I thought for one happy moment that I was getting away with it. She appeared to be walking straight past me. When she was about four yards away, however, she seemed to change her mind. She looked hard at me and said: 'I must tell you this . . .'

'No, Ethel! I'm sorry but I'm terribly busy, can't stop, luv.'

'But I must tell you . . .' she repeated, staring straight at me.

'No! I'll call tomorrow and see you, I promise.'

I sidestepped Ethel and increased my pace and my perspiration.

The heat was stifling. I turned into Danby Row and removed my helmet. Danby Row had been a Victorian two-up and two-down street but had been allowed to run to seed after the war. It had been completely demolished with the exception of two houses, the occupiers of which had refused to move to the nearby huge housing estates. Corrugated iron sheeting ran along both sides of the street like a small polished ravine. There were three or four abandoned motor vehicles in the road and each of them had been cannibalized by motorists for spares. I saw a figure kneeling down at the side of an old Vauxhall car. He was slackening the wheel-nut.

He looked up at my approach, then with some effort climbed slowly to his feet. He was a huge slob of a man, aged about thirty-five. His trousers were belted tightly under a beer-belly. A filthy singlet partially covered his chest and most of the flesh that could be seen was covered by an assortment of rather badly worked and obscene tattoos. He was grossly overweight and his lank hair hung down to his shoulders in greasy black clusters. I had never seen him before but I felt an instant dislike for him. He looked the type of person that God created for that sole purpose. I found that my abhorrence of him was almost therapeutic. I disliked him so much I was beginning to feel better. He sauntered towards me. The leer on his face showed his discoloured and broken teeth to their most effective advantage. He stopped about a yard away and directly in front of me.

''Ere, John!' he smirked.

'What do you want?' I answered curtly, calling upon the

full dignity of the law. I eyed him with what I hoped passed for a cool withering stare.

'Yer flies are undone!' Then he turned and went back to the car, never giving me as much as a second glance.

Panic-stricken, I looked down. There must have been five buttons showing. A torn shirt, no helmet and my flies undone! I must look an absolute picture. My buttons must have ripped open when I fell into that stinking room. I had been up and down that ladder, I had been talking to neighbours, I had been giving orders and finally I had walked the streets, all with my Marks and Spencers Y-fronts tantalizingly exposed. Heaven above knows what I must have looked like with just one shoe on and my modesty almost bared. I mumbled some thanks and fumbled with my fingers until the last button was secure. I replaced my helmet and slunk the remaining streets to Wharf Road Police Station.

I walked into the front office and the first person I saw was Bernadette. She looked up from her writings.

'A thousand dead rats to you, Harry,' she said simply and sweetly.

'Yes, sorry about that, Bernadette, but I have not had a good day,' I answered.

'Do you know your shirt is torn and your back is grazed – bloody hell!! – what on earth is that smell?' she exclaimed.

'I'm afraid it's me,' I said apologetically.

Inspector Lisle looked up from his ancient typewriter. He had been composing a one-fingered correspondence ever since I had left the station, two hours previously.

'Well make out your report double-quick, then piss off home. You'll make us all puke!'

'Thanks, sir, you're a real sweety,' I said in a voice that was supposed to be jocular. In reality I could have cut his throat.

The problem was where to go to write out my report. The favourite spot was usually the canteen but it was lunchtime. If I went in there smelling like this I would get lynched – or buried. I eventually found an empty office where the typists had gone to lunch and hastily completed my paper work. I quickly gave it to the station officer together with £721.

'Haven't you got a plastic bag to put that money in? It stinks,' called Lisle.

'Miss Morton had no traceable next-of-kin and this money will all go to the state,' I answered. 'I consider that for £721 the state can provide its own plastic bags.'

One hour later, I had plunged all of my clothing into two buckets of disinfectant and I was wallowing in a cool bath. I glanced down at my wrist and I was aware that I had forgotten to remove my wrist-watch. I dried my hands, undid the strap and placed the watch carefully on the bathroom stool. As I did so I was aware of a black stain on my wrist immediately underneath the spot that my watch had been covering. I reached for the soap. Suddenly the stain fell from my wrist and struggled in the bath-water! I fetched both hands down with a resounding 'thwack' on to the surface of the foam. Water went everywhere! In the stool, the cabinet, all over the floor and up my nose, but I could not see where the creature went.

I eventually dried myself and raided my daughter's perfumery. I emerged from the bathroom smelling like a Hollywood whorehouse. My wife had by now arrived home from work and was downstairs in the kitchen making tea.

'Hullo, darling,' she greeted me. 'You are home early. Good God! What on earth is that smell?'

I slumped down on a kitchen chair. Oh what a day!

Why the hell did I ever join the police force?

2. Training School

I had left the army in 1950 having reached the rank of private. I was engaged to be married and I needed a job. The clerk at the labour exchange suggested one of the government-sponsored training centres, where skills and trades are taught in a crash course of two to three years.

'Which trade d'you recommend?' I asked.

'Take my tip, son, become a stone-mason. There'll always be work for stone-masons. Always 'as been, ever since the Stone Age.'

Well, I've been looking for him ever since.

I became a mason and eventually joined twenty-seven other craftsmen in a stone yard at Battersea. Within two and a half years we were all redundant. I sometimes feel quite guilty about this. Civilization has been building with stone for six thousand years. Yet two years after I pick up my first mallet and chisel, the whistle goes for time. An experience like that does tend to sap one's confidence. The writing on the wall had become so obvious that it was almost hand-carved. I needed another job, but what?

Whilst perusing the football results one September evening, I saw an ad for the Metropolitan Police. I spent Sunday considering its implications and discussing it with my wife and by that evening my application was in the post.

In late October, I was asked to attend for a medical at Beak Street Recruiting Centre, just a short distance from Piccadilly. A most peculiar examination took place. At no time during this interview was I within three yards of the doctor. I took off all my clothes and stood across the room from him.

'Show me the backs of your hands,' was the somewhat surprising request.

I complied.

'H'mmm,' he murmured.

Whenever I hear a doctor say 'H'mmm' I am convinced I have but days to live.

'Have you ever had piles?'

I immediately brightened. Piles may be very unpleasant but they certainly were not terminal and in any case, I did not suffer from them.

'Er, no,' I said, rapidly looking down to my hands and wondering what the connection could be between the two extremities.

'Good, good. All right, you can dress now.'

'Is that all?' I asked a little incredulously, still staring at my hands.

'Yes,' he replied in an acid tone. 'Why, would you like something serious?'

'No, no, sir,' I stammered. 'No thank you very much.'

I had, after all, lost a day's work for this examination and building workers did not get paid for time lost, particularly for interviews for another job. As far as I could ascertain, all that I had achieved for the loss of a day's wages was the knowledge that I had nice hands and no piles. A high price to pay.

The following week, I was obliged to lose another day's work, again to Beak Street, this time for a written exam and an interview. The examination was the customary Civil Service third-class entrance paper and I found it fairly straightforward. The interview, however, was mildly surprising. I was shown into a room with four very senior-looking police officers who sat in pairs behind two desks. Apart from the obviously expected question – 'Why do you wish to join?' – countered by the obviously expected answer – 'I like meeting people' (does anyone ever say anything different?) – I was a little surprised to be asked: 'What paper do you read?'

I thought of lying and saying *The Times* but my nerve broke and I said, 'The *Daily Herald*' (now, alas, defunct).

'Do you read it all, or just the sports pages?'

'Every single word, sir, that's why I buy it' (a blatant lie).

One of the elderly gentlemen on the board then said, rather sharply: 'Are you joining the police just for the pay?'

'No, sir,' I answered very quickly, 'in fact I'm taking a £2 per week reduction in wages.'

This was obviously his stock question, because he clammed up immediately and never uttered another word throughout the rest of the interview.

'Have you ever committed an offence, however small, against the law?' said another.

I paused for a moment and decided to substitute 'being found out' for 'committed' and happily answered, 'No.'

Great play was then made of the first job that I had after I had left school. I was fourteen at the time and I had worked for four months, but apparently the firm had kept no record of me. This was quite a blow to my morale. I had honestly believed that I had been indispensable. But soon the questions lapsed, and I was dismissed. Two weeks later I received my enrolling date. I was finally on my way. Monday, 1 December 1952, found me walking into Peel House, the Metropolitan Police Training School near Victoria, to begin my twelve-week training course. Peel House was an old nineteenth-century building which, in those days, took in half of the police recruits in London. In the mid-1960s the Metropolitan Police was dragged reluctantly and at times almost screamingly into the twentieth century. But in 1952 nothing much had really changed in the force since Sir Robert Peel's day. If the force itself had not changed, then the training school and its methods had remained equally static.

The early fifties were not part of the Dark Ages. Yet at Peel House, a training school for one of the largest bodies of police in the world, in one of the greatest cities in the world, we were learning about such handy subjects as 'sheep-dipping', 'Epizootic-lymphangitis' (a *very* rare animal disease) and how to stop a runaway horse! The first rule for stopping this animal was an absolute gem. It read: 'First run in the same direction as the horse.' It made no mention about running any faster!

Classes at Peel House consisted of twenty recruits and an instructor. The course was divided into three four-week periods. At the end of each of these four weeks, the instructors would change around and a revision test was held. If a recruit failed any of the revision tests, or fell sick, then he or she was 'back-squadded', that is, placed into the class behind. Intakes into the school entered every two weeks and a recruit could only be back-squadded once. To fail two revision tests meant – out.

The sleeping arrangements were based on the pre-war section house system: one long room, partitioned off into bed-spaces by a plywood screen, about seven feet high, all around the bed and locker. There was a gap under each partition, about a foot high, and if anything was dropped, it always rolled at least two bed spaces away. The two girls in our class were, needless to say, spirited away each evening to a policewoman's hostel somewhere in the West End. Fun was frowned upon at Peel House. On the third night at the school, I was awakened by the sound of sobbing, seemingly in the same room as myself. I eventually stood up on my bed and peered over the partition. I saw Andy McEvoy, a slim curly-haired Scot and a Korean war veteran, lying in his bed and whimpering. I quietly called down: 'What's the matter, Andy?'

He instantly stopped crying and turned sharply over and faced the opposite wall to me. Nothing I could say would induce him to speak. He never arrived for breakfast that morning and at lunchtime I heard that he had returned home to Dumfries. Peel House had a most unpredictable effect on the most stable of people.

Classes began at 9 a.m. and officially ended at 5 p.m. but most of us were still in the classrooms until lights out at 11 p.m. I found the three months that I spent at training school a period of almost unrelieved gloom. Mind you, the weather did nothing to help. The winter of 1952/3 was the foggiest in living memory and on many days vast areas of London were totally paralysed for the whole of the twenty-four hours. Old people, and young ones too, for that matter, were dying in hundreds. The dense grey smog was like a stagnant sea. It descended so thickly that it didn't even swirl. Sounds were muted, or non-existent. Boats and trains ceased to run. Weeks became just a fusion of days and nights, without dusks or dawns to divide them.

They were the twelve hardest weeks of my life. The instructors crammed us full of legal knowledge, first-aid and self-defence. For about a month after the end of the course I could dress a pelvic fracture; 'throw' a drunken sixteen-stone navvy over my shoulder, and feel like the Solicitor General in my knowledge of Gladstone's Criminal Law Amendment Act of 1871. I was, however, totally incapable of retaining all of these facts and I had forgotten most of them within weeks of leaving the training school.

This was, to my mind, the greatest mistake of the Peel

House system: it tried to pack so much legal knowledge into such a short duration that few individuals could retain their grasp of the law for any worthwhile period. It was simply not possible subsequently to achieve the same mastery of the law outside on the streets that one had shown a few weeks previously in the classroom. When a recruit left Peel House he was expected to decide instantly in a street situation: *(a)* which party had violated the law; *(b)* which law had been violated; and *(c)* whether there was a power of arrest for the offence committed. Just the sort of legal niceties that a QC can peruse in his chambers for a couple of hours or so in the course of an evening, with every law book at hand.

Foot drill was another aspect touched on at the school, but with no great enthusiasm. For some reason that I have never been able to understand, a marching body of police always looks a shambles. There is no logical explanation for this. Eighteen out of twenty in the class had been in the Services, yet when it came to marching we were a disaster.

Most instructors at the period had seen service in one or other branches of the armed forces, and Peel House tended to be run somewhat like an army training camp. It taught law and discipline but very little else. In those days, the other half of the police intake went to the police training school at Hendon, where attitudes seemed more in keeping with the times. All recruits, nowadays, go to the Peel Centre at Hendon, where the first basic steps as a policeman are taken in circumstances that have changed out of all recognition.

For instance, other than the weekend leave and the weekly swim at the municipal baths at Victoria, we never set foot outside the building. In theory, any student could go out pleasure-bent in the evenings. In practice, however, the requirements of the course were too demanding to permit this. The result of this system was to make the training school very insular. I never learnt about functions of any of our allied services. I never had a talk from a fireman, or saw an ambulance. I never spoke to a doctor, or visited a hospital casualty. They did, however, show us the film *Blue Lamp*. This starred the actor Jack Warner as an old policeman and was classified then as a training film!

One exception to this rule came in the seventh week of our service. The door of our classroom was hurled open and in roared Superintendent Tommy Daw. Daw was the roughest of diamonds and a big man in every sense of the word. His bellowing voice could always be heard throughout the building, as he cursed and yelled at an endless string of 'bloody incompetent twits'. He breathed fire and brimstone, yet he was grudgingly admired by most. Like the majority of recruits of that period, I had had experience of company sergeant-majors in the army, so perhaps for me a little of Daw's sting was removed. However the few girls who joined the force in those days did not have this advantage to fall back on, and it was no exaggeration to say that Tommy Daw would simply reduce them to tears.

This particular morning, Daw exploded into our classroom. Instinct caused most of the male members of the class to leap immediately to their feet. The two girls were slower. One, in fact, barely moved at all. Daw swung round on them.

'What's the matter wiv you two? Got glue in your drawers? Git up when a senior officer enters!'

The girls rocketed to their feet. I looked at our instructor, Sergeant McPhee. He had momentarily closed his eyes, as if in disbelief.

'You are all going out lunchtime,' said Daw, 'you are going down to Victoria mortuary. If you are going to faint at the sight of a dead body, then you had better faint while you are here, at Training School, rather than out on the streets. Because if you faint on the streets, then the ambulance crew may be tempted to pick up the wrong body.'

With that he turned sharply and stumped out of the room, slamming the door behind him.

There was a clatter as nearly everyone sat down. I say 'nearly' because Julia Kirby was standing rigid, her face changed with chameleon-like rapidity, from crimson to ashen grey.

'You can sit down now, Miss Kirby,' said Sergeant McPhee.

Julia moved just her eyes; she turned them towards him. 'Sergeant, I – I just cannot look at a dead body.'

Brenda Johnson reached up and slowly but firmly pulled Julia down to a sitting position.

'But surely you thought about this before you joined?' said McPhee.

'No, I just somehow hoped that I would never have to do it,' she whispered.

At 1.20 p.m., immediately after shepherd's pie, bread pudding and custard, the class assembled in the foyer at Peel House and walked in twos and threes down Regency Street, towards the mortuary. The fogs of December and January had reluctantly abated but the aftermath could be seen everywhere. A film of black mud covered everything that had been exposed to the elements. The grass on the nearby playing fields appeared to be a shiny grey in colour. Vehicle lights penetrated the early afternoon gloom as they swished towards Victoria. The drizzle was so fine that it did not seem to be falling at all; it was just there, suspended five feet above pavement level. Just one more misery to be braved by pedestrians as they scurried about their daily business.

The rest of the population may have been 'scurrying' but those twenty recruits, about to enter their first mortuary stood out as the slowest walkers seen in London all day. We had been told to walk in twos and threes but the herd instinct prevailed. Within two minutes we had become a solid bunch, twenty strong, walking on each other's heels and bouncing from each other's shoulders. The reason being that this was our first venture on the streets in uniform and we were as self-conscious as nuns in a brothel.

We were in something of a dilemma on the walk. None of us wished to be the first in the mortuary but neither did any of us wish to be last. One always had the feeling that some member of the public was rushing along Regency Street looking for a policeman and if you were the last in line, then it could just be you. We walked with our gaze straight ahead, making nervous little jokes to each other, until we all finally assembled on the forecourt of Victoria mortuary.

I stared at the door in total disbelief. It was a massive wooden structure with huge iron hinges and the most colossal and ornate knocker that I had ever seen. I just *had* to be the one to knock. I lifted up the bottom of the knocker and fetched it down on the base as hard as I could. What satisfaction! The crash reverberated from the door and up the entire length of my arm. The babble of our group ceased at the majesty of that knock.

'I bet the door creaks,' said a prophetic female voice from somewhere behind me.

Exactly on this cue, the door was slowly opened by a deathly pale youth in an ill-fitting jacket and even the noise of the passing traffic paled beside the groaning of those magnificent hinges.

'Do come in, I'th been exthpecting you all,' said the lisping youth.

I felt I should look quickly around for Count Dracula. At first, I could not take my eyes from the mortuary attendant. He was about twenty years old, five feet ten inches tall, with thin wispy fair hair; he was very slim with sharp features; his teeth, though good in colour, protruded slightly over his bottom lip. His suit appeared to be much too small for him and he spoke in a soft, almost effeminate way.

'We've had a bit of a clear-out thith morning, tho everyone'th got room to breath, tho to thpeak,' he laughed nervously.

I realized that he was only nervous of our presence; he was most certainly not nervous of his job – in fact he revelled in it.

He led us along an echoing corridor, past several insignificant-looking portals, until we came to a double door at the end of the passageway.

'Here, tho to thpeak, ith where it all happenth,' said our guide.

He dramatically threw open the doors and there was a large room, measuring about forty feet by twenty feet. The floor consisted of small ceramic black and white tiles, the surface sloped gently to the right, towards a gully which disappeared into a small drain. Four empty stone tables lay in a straight line across the room. Each table had a stone pillow with a concave centre and red rubber sheet folded neatly across its base.

'We're a bit thlack now. Everyone'th gone to lunch,' said the attendant.

'Jesus Christ! Do you feed 'em?' exclaimed Peter Ward.

'In fact we're not buthy at all. During the fogth of a month ago, we had them thtanding round the wallth, tho to thpeak. But jutht come and have a look at thith.'

With that, our attendant led the way to the far wall and for the first time I noticed that three of the walls appeared to consist of a double line of large filing cabinets. He pulled open one of the drawers and the naked head and torso of a slightly built man in his sixties slid into view. The dead man had a large hole in the centre of his forehead.

'You know who thith ith don't you?'

'No,' several of us chorused.

'Yeth you do!' His voice had risen an octave.

'No,' we murmured again, uncertain this time as we gathered round for a better view; but no matter how we looked at the corpse, no famous name came to mind.

'It'th our mortuary attendant!' he exclaimed. 'He'th wound up in hith own bloody mortuary! He got knocked down by a lorry going home latht night!'

There was a slight thud from the back of the group as Julia Kirby slumped to the floor in a dead faint. Several of the fellows rushed to assist her. Julia was quite a buxom girl and one of the rules we had recently learnt for dealing with fainting was to loosen the patient's clothing. Brenda Johnson, however, remained a true friend; snubbing any suggestion of heart massage, she slowly assisted Julia to regain consciousness. Now if I learnt one thing at all in my three months at the Training School, it was never let a patient regain consciousness in a mortuary, even if they are amongst friends. Julia's screams must have been heard half-way to Hampstead. After ten minutes in the attendant's rest-room and half-a-cup of his awful tea, she claimed to be fit enough to return to Peel House. It was some indication of the way the poor girl felt, that she was happier facing Tommy Daw than spending another minute in that building. That, then, was our only excursion away from the precincts of Training School. Hardly an unqualified success.

The eighth week at the school saw the customary revision

test. This stage of the course featured the reporting of traffic accidents. These incidents were reported in a yellow booklet. Because of the complexities of some accidents, a great deal of information was required. Many a recruit came to grief at this stage and it was not without reason that the booklets were often referred to as 'Yellow Perils'. Accidents were 'set up' in the school yard, with instructors acting usually as truculent members of the public. Two very old Standard Eight motor cars were kept for this purpose (neither of them had been capable of being driven for many years). They would be pushed into each other and both 'drivers' would proceed to argue violently, each blaming the other for the accident.

Great play was rightly made in these exercises of finding out as soon as possible *exactly* what had taken place. Each recruit would say in parrot fashion: 'What has happened here, sir, please?' If he felt by the information offered to him that subsequent court action may arise, he was further instructed to ask loudly: 'Did anyone see what happened?' This was a good baptism into the waters of indifference, because usually no witness would volunteer to come forward. It would then be up to the recruit to dig and pry and eventually find out for himself just what had happened. This could be done by the position of the vehicles, statements of the drivers and perhaps by any damage that was caused. In no accident which either I or my class-mates were involved was a witness ever forthcoming; that is, with one exception.

Builders were working at the school at the time, extending one of the classrooms. The yard, which had little space at the best of times, became quite hazardous with scaffolding and piles of rubble scattered everywhere. Two instructors set up a 'collision' by using the rubble as an obstruction, the allegation being that one of the drivers swerved very late around the pile and left the other driver insufficient time to take any avoiding action. Both cars were pushed into suitable 'collision positions' and Julia Kirby was asked to deal with the incident. The rest of us watched.

Julia's 'What has happened here, sir, please?' was greeted with customary animosity by both 'drivers'. Eventually, Julia got around to asking the follow-up question: 'Did anyone see what happened?' and for the first time I heard a reply.

'Oi did, Miss! Oi did indeed! Dat sergeant dere, pushed dat car dere, into the front of de odder car. And I tink he did it for der purpose.'

We all looked up for the voice and there on the scaffolding stood an indignant, red-haired, donkey-jacketed building worker, who had obviously been watching the whole proceedings with great interest. Julia adjusted well, I thought. She simply took a statement from the labourer, cautioned the instructor and then told him that she was arresting him for malicious damage! This worked extremely well, a mock court was set up in the classroom the following morning and our defendant was fined thirty bob! The whole class learned more from that than any other comparable lesson we had in the school.

As the course built up to the final month, there seemed to be more and more laws, facts, drills and school-yard demonstrations to attend to. I had just about answered enough questions in the first-aid exam to have scraped through. This was followed the same afternoon by our test on reporting accidents. This time, however, there would be no Irish witnesses to assist. We were strictly on our own. The accident would be set up and we would be sent for individually and alphabetically. Once we had finished the test we would be segregated into a spare classroom so that no information could filter back to those still to be tested.

I was the third on the scene and Superintendent Daw was the examining officer. One of the Standard motor cars was positioned half-way across the mock pavement, an instructor lay partially underneath the car. A large wooden pole lay on the ground, adjacent to the front near-side wheel. Daw pointed to the wooden pole and said: 'This lamp post has been knocked down by the car which has mounted the pavement. It has also run over this unfortunate man. Over to you, PC Cole.'

My first reaction was one of mild joy. It could have been much worse. Perhaps a three-vehicle pile-up, or a horse knocked down, or even a bus tragedy. It would be safe to say that I was quite pleased with my 'accident'. Not much to do here, except remove the injured man to hospital and inform the electricity board about the lamp post. The victim groaned in mock agony. Of course, the Training School's golden rule! – 'Take care of the injured first.'

I knelt beside the man, oozing confidence.

'Where is the pain, sir?'

'My legs, officer. They hurt something cruel.'

I nobly placed my coat over him.

'Could I have a fag, officer?'

Crafty sod, I thought. I bet he cadges cigarettes from every student on the test. Must be quite profitable with twenty in the class. Well it *was* an exam and I did not wish to upset one of the examiners. If he wanted a 'fag' he should have one. I inserted a Players Weight into his lips and lit a match.

'BANG! BANG! BLOODY BANG!' yelled Tommy Daw. 'You've killed yourself, the victim, five elderly by-standers and a Mother Superior who was passing by. You've blown them all up, you bloody incompetent twit!'

'But, but – how, sir?' I bleated.

'Bloody fractured gas pipe! Gas is everywhere and you cheerfully light bloody matches!'

'But how was I to know that it was a gas lamp? I thought it was electricity.'

'Look here, you twit,' shouted Daw. He rolled the 'lamp post' over with his foot. Written in the palest of blue chalk, on the underside of the pole, in letters not one inch high, was the word 'GAS'.

The instructor happily puffed on my cigarette as I dejectedly trooped off to the classroom where the testees were to wait. I cheered up to find that the two students already there had also blown up their patient. Every five minutes or so, the door would open and a forlorn figure would slink in muttering remarks like: 'I've just blown up half London and it cost me a fag.' Tommy Daw certainly knew how to get a point over.

Three weeks later the final exams were held. Sixteen of us passed and we were given a week's leave. We would not know what division we would be posted to until we returned after that leave. We said our temporary farewells and wished luck to the unfortunate four who were back-squadded. They would have to sit the exam again in two weeks' time.

I packed my holdall and left the school. I decided to walk into Parliament Square to catch the bus home. I could have caught another bus from almost outside the Training School but Parliament Square in those days had about six policemen working an elaborate traffic point. I wanted to watch them; soon that would be me. Perhaps I would look after Winston Churchill at 10 Downing Street; or the new Queen at Buckingham Palace. I began to cross Whitehall; I waited beside a tall 'A' Division policeman for the traffic to pass. He looked perished, his nose seemed to dominate his whole face and it was running red with the cold. It suddenly dawned on me that never in my whole life had I ever spoken to a real live policeman. The Training School instructors did not seem to count somehow. I decided now would be as good a time as any to put that right.

'Hullo,' I said, somewhat weakly. 'I've just joined the force.'

He looked down at me for some seconds and, cuffing his nose on his traffic gauntlet, said: 'Then you must be pissed!'

I detected a slight mist on my rose-coloured glasses.

3. Learning Beats

The week slipped by very quickly and soon we reassembled at Peel House. We each received our postings and said our goodbyes. Twenty young people went off to police the same city; twelve of them I never saw again.

I received my posting to 'L' division together with Jimmy Davenport and Peter Ward. Later that morning we arrived at Brixton Police Station, which was the 'L' Division HQ. Peter Ward was to remain at Brixton while Jimmy Davenport and I were posted about three miles away to the sub-divisional station of Wharf Road.

I was unhappy on two counts. First, Wharf Road was almost home to me. I lived on number twelve beat and did not relish the idea of policing my own neighbourhood. City policemen rarely do. The second reason was Jimmy Davenport. In modern parlance he would be classified as 'gay'. In those days he was simply referred to as 'Doris'.

Jimmy was a tall, good-looking lad of twenty years. His movements were feminine and graceful, his complexion all peaches and cream, and he was one of God's gentle creatures. I liked him very much but I was not pleased to be part of a twosome. Jimmy did nothing to help my feelings with his eternal singing. He had quite a pleasant voice but he always sang girls' songs. His favourite at that time was entitled 'Men are Good for Nothing'. Some years after he had resigned from the force I heard him singing in a strip-club in Denman Street. As a singer he was fair, as a friend he was good, as a policeman he could be an embarrassment.

Monday afternoon found us having a brief interview with the Wharf Road superintendent. He gave us the usual 'welcome aboard' speech. '. . . and if there is anything I can do for you – *anything* at all! Just let me know. My door is always open to my men,' he concluded in loving tones.

I did in fact go to see him some months later with a desperate housing problem. I couldn't get into his 'always open door' for close on three days and when I did, he said: 'D'yer think I've got sod-all else to do but wet-nurse you? I've got problems of my own, y'know.'

I was informed by the superintendent's clerk that I would be learning beats for a month and I was to be posted night-duty for the rest of the week. I would start my first tour of duty the following day – Tuesday. I had collected the rest of my clothing from the stores and I made my way home with two tunics, two pairs of trousers, two helmets, one ceremonial outfit, one pair of leggings, overcoat, raincoat, cape, truncheon and innumerable books and forms. This presented no little storage problem. My wife and I lived in a small two-roomed basement flat with no cupboards!

It was true to say that I was disappointed with my posting to 'L' division. I had hoped to go to West End Central, Hyde Park, or somewhere that at least had a football stadium. But 'L' division had all of the disadvantages of London with none of its rewards. Brixton, Peckham, Clapham, Camberwell, but the least desirable of all these stations was Wharf Road.

The station was situated in the thoroughfare of Wharf Road, within the Borough of Southwark. It was built towards the end of the last century and was one of the more modern buildings in the neighbourhood. It was a densely populated area and included numerous small streets, many of which had remained flattened since the blitz some ten years earlier. It was the part of London I knew best and liked least. I was born and raised there. For the next twenty-five years I was to have a love-hate relationship with it. Somehow I never managed to get myself out of it. It had always abounded with saints and sinners and I could never make up my mind which I wanted to be.

After a sleepless day I cycled into the station yard ready to report for my first night-duty. I knew the times of the three duties as 6 a.m.–2 p.m. early, 2 p.m.–10 p.m. late, and 10 p.m.–6 a.m. nights. I brushed myself down and walked into the front office.

Sergeant 'Billy' Budd was the station officer and he was sitting at a desk with a typewriter in front of him. Every two or three seconds he would strike a key with a thick sausage-like finger, his tongue wrapped around his top lip in grim determination. Each thud on the keys would shake the desk. I stood slightly to one side, wondering what to say and why there were so few policemen about. The only other occupants of the front office were a bald, middle-aged policeman, tapping out a message on a teleprinter, and a quaint-looking elderly woman, who sat at a switchboard knitting furiously. She wore a large green eye-shade.

I looked back at the station officer. I saw that the carriage of the typewriter was laboriously making its way to the end of its run. I also noticed that it was about to push over a cup of tea that was placed on the desk alongside. I was just too late. With yet one more almighty thud, Bill banged out another letter and flooded his desk. Tea was everywhere. The very important-looking documents lying on the desk took on the hue of weak custard. Bill threw back his head in disgust.

'Aw f—' he stopped in mid oath as he noticed me for the first time.

'What d'you want?' he asked aggressively.

'I'm – er – I'm learning beats, sergeant,' I answered apologetically.

'What shift?' said Bill sharply.

'Nights, sergeant,' I replied, thinking that it must have been obvious.

'Why are you late?' he snapped.

I looked up at the office clock. It read exactly 10 p.m.

'I didn't think I was. It's only just ten now,' I said anxiously.

'Didn't you know that you are supposed to parade fifteen minutes before the hour on whatever duty you are required to perform?' he recited.

'No. Why?'

'To acquaint yourself, lad, to acquaint yourself!' he yelled.

I pointed out that I thought this was a rotten idea and if we had been required to start fifteen minutes early without pay in the building trade, we would have all been on strike in a flash. He in his turn pointed out that although I was no longer in the building trade, if I reported for duty at 10 p.m. anymore I might find myself back there. Furthermore, if I had been on any other duty than nights, I would have been sent home to report in eight hours' time for the next shift.

This was one police regulation that I really resented. I once worked out that because of it the Commissioner of Police received three months' extra service out of me, without payment, during my time in the force.

'Well you're too late to go out with any of the night-duty, they have all left for their beats. Stay in the front office and help me. You can go out with the first man who returns to the station,' said Bill.

'Yes, sergeant. What do you want me to do?'

'Can you bloody-well type?'

'No.'

'Then look after that counter and deal with the customers. I don't want to see anyone, no one at all. *And* I don't want any interruptions, understand?'

Bill showed he considered the audience at an end by placing a fresh sheet of paper in the typewriter and muttering to himself.

I realized in the next couple of years that Bill was a great mutterer. He always tried to be fierce to recruits but was seen through instantly. He would look at you for a few seconds and then, as if in apology for his outburst, would begin to mutter to himself in his strong Yorkshire accent. He was over six feet in height and of good physique. His thick wavy hair was iron-grey and his face would break into a wide grin at the slightest provocation. He had no fear of physical matters but he did not relish verbal confrontation. He had been a commando during the war and, I would guess, enjoyed it immensely. He liked a drink but two pints would render him incoherent. Three would paralyse him. He was one of the most likeable people I ever met in my life and I consider I was fortunate to be under his wing for the first two years in the force.

I spent the next ninety minutes apprehensively at the counter, although most of the dozen or so people who came in had quite straightforward problems. Lost dogs, lost cycles, lost people and a taxi-driver who had found a ferret in his cab. If there were any problems at all, then I tip-toed past Bill and asked George Perrin, who had by now finished his teleprinter broadcast. I had just begun to think I was getting the hang of this counter-work, when in she came.

My attention was drawn first by the clip-clop of heels on the polished wood blocks of the entrance-hall floor. I looked up to see a 'lady of the night' striding determinedly towards my counter. The Salvation Army may have referred to these ladies as 'fallen women' but this girl was the most wholesome-looking creature I had ever seen. Vitality shone from every pore. But I had never seen anyone looking so angry.

Rosie was small, a little over five feet perhaps. Her lack of height was somewhat offset by her jet-black hair. It was swept up into an enormous dark wave, the peak of which was nine inches above her forehead. Her dark eyes were heavily mascara'd; her full lips were thickly painted and exaggerated into a large bow, which almost touched the bottom of her snub nose. Her teeth had a couple of gaps but were of a good white. She wore a white, long-sleeved, satin blouse; a pencil-slim gabardine knee-length skirt, tightly belted at the waist; straight black seamed stockings; and very high heels with an ankle strap.

The most spectacular aspect of Rosie, however, was her breasts. They were not over large, yet as she strode quickly across the hall they appeared to be nodding in turn. I found great difficulty in avoiding nodding back.

'Er, yes, Miss?' I said somewhat weakly.

'I've been assaulted. In fact I've been *indecently* assaulted. Oh, and robbed,' she snapped, as an after-thought.

'How? Where? Who by?' I said, attempting to put on an official manner and hoping I sounded like a detective.

'By this sodding punter, of course!' she screamed. 'Oh gawd! Look, I ain't talking to no boys, goan git me a copper,' she added.

I could feel myself colouring. Suddenly she looked past me and saw the station officer.

'Ullo, Bill. Fank gawd you're 'ere.'

Bill rose to his feet, his face opened into a huge grin.

'Wassamatter, Rosie?'

I wondered fleetingly how they knew each other.

'A bleedin' punter's bit my Bristols. And it bleedin' 'urts,' she exclaimed.

'Well let's have a look, Rosie, love,' said Bill.

There was a scrambling noise from the vicinity of the teleprinter as George Perrin searched desperately for his glasses.

Without more ado Rosie unbuttoned her blouse to reveal a slightly less than white, size thirty-six 'C'-cup bra. She quickly slipped the strap from her right shoulder. There, peeping out at two pleasantly surprised members of the constabulary, was a rather attractive right breast.

'Hmmmmmmmmmmm,' said Bill.

He reached out and lifted it slightly. I thought at first he was weighing it.

'Unblemished!' he stated. 'Tell you what, Rosie, get the other one out and we can see if there is any swelling,' he added.

With little ado, two more buttons popped, a quick shrug of the shoulder and Rosie looked like 'Venus emerging from a police station counter'. This time Bill appeared to weigh both. He seemed quite happy with the weight of them and turned to me and said:

'What d'you think, lad?'

'I – I, think they look very nice, sergeant,' I stammered.

'Hear that, Rosie? This young man thinks they look very nice. So do I. Put them away now, there's a good girl.'

An oath from the corner of the office caused me to relinquish my gaze at the fair Rosie. I saw that George Perrin had now discovered his glasses – but sadly too late.

'Well, Rosie, I'm afraid we can't take any action on this. It's what we call a common assault. You could take out a summons yourself. What was the robbery you mentioned?'

Rosie now seemed more tranquil. She had the solemn word of two police officers that her 'Bristols' had lost none of their old charm and things obviously did not seem so bad.

'The bastard must 'ave nicked the fiver he paid me while I was running cold-water over me "nellies".'

'D'you know who he was?' said Bill.

Instantly Rosie erupted again.

'Do I know who he was? Do I know who he was?' she repeated. 'If I fuckin' well knew that, I would not have come all the fuckin' way down here to see you silly pair of sods! I would 'ave castrated the fucker! Men, you're all alike! You're all so fuckin' unprincipled!'

With that she turned on the points of her heels, tossed her head and clip-clopped down the passage. Bill and I watched her until she disappeared out into the night.

'Is it like this very often, sergeant?' I asked rather hopefully, turning to Bill.

'Not on a Tuesday, son, not on a Tuesday, well – not as a rule.'

A few minutes later, the first returning member of the night-duty ventured back into the station. This introduced me to surely the most archaic practice that any profession has ever acquired – the ritual of book ninety-two.

It was a discipline offence in those days to be found within the confines of the station building without either permission or a very good reason. (The forty-five-minute meal break of course excepted.) Tea was usually made around midnight and again at 4 a.m. At these times men would begin to wander back to the station. However, a tea break was most certainly against the discipline code. This is where book ninety-two came in. No constable was allowed to enter the station premises without making an entry in that book. It listed three column headings:

Under the first column would be inserted 'Toilet' or 'WC'. The times usually shown were 12 night – 12.10 a.m. and 4 a.m. – 4.10 a.m.

The same procedure would apply on all three shifts. The early turn would venture in for tea about 7.30 a.m., which was just before the traffic-points began, and again about mid-day. The late turn would arrive back about 3.15 p.m., just before the schools emptied, and again about 8 p.m. With three shifts operating at each station, this form of punctual dysentery attacked six times per day, 365 days of the year. No commercial laxative could claim such regularity. One night's work by the 'Angel of Death' caused the Jews to celebrate the Passover for more than three thousand years. Book ninety-two hit the Metropolitan Police six times daily for over a century and until now it has never rated a mention. There is no doubt but that it's not what you know but Who you know.

At 12.10 a.m. I left Wharf Road Police Station in company with PC Brian Smiley. Brian was a nice enough lad but he didn't talk. It was a bit like taking your dog for a walk. We strolled throughout the night through scores of deserted streets and alleys and he barely uttered a dozen words. He was supposed to point out such things as vulnerable properties, the homes and haunts of known villains and any of a thousand-and-one details that may be of use to a recruit. All he said was, 'I'd like to leave the police and grow flowers in the Scilly Isles.' And that was it. Fortunately, being a local boy, I knew the area better than he did. He was the shyest bloke I ever met. The night dragged and at 6.00 a.m. I wearily cycled home.

It was the first time that I had ever worked through the night. I found it most unnatural and never once became used to it. If working at night was difficult, then sleeping during the day was usually impossible. Our basement flat nestled neatly over the Northern Line on one of London's busiest Underground tracks. Every few minutes throughout the day the whole flat vibrated as Piccadilly-bound commuters thundered beneath my bed. In the interval between trains, cars would screech to a halt at the pedestrian crossing outside our front door. I tossed and turned and after five hours of being neither asleep nor awake, I finally left my bed for an afternoon breakfast.

I arrived at Wharf Road in ample time, 9.35 p.m. in fact. Not that I was very happy about that. I had never been early for work in my life and I did not care for the new experience. Station sergeant Wally Down had returned from a weekly leave and Billy Budd took up the job of section sergeant. (George Perrin had mentioned that after last night's experience with Rosie, he should have been called 'sexual' sergeant.) This entailed supervising the men on the beat and getting the shift ready for the duty officer to inspect. Each shift had an inspector in charge and usually two sergeants working under him. In addition there would be a station sergeant in control of the front office.

Inspector McLeod was our duty officer. If he had one obsession, other than scotch, it was recruits. He would breathe whisky fumes all over you as he asked where had you been, where were you going, why were you going there anyway? If breathalysers had been inaugurated fifteen years earlier, he would have been done twice nightly with a matinee on Saturdays. The infuriating thing was that he had a God-given gift for always catching recruits out. He knew every dodge in the book. I didn't like him, I didn't respect him, and I considered him a drunken devious bastard, but I had to admire him. Of all the hundreds of supervising officers I subsequently met, none of them nailed me down as completely as McLeod.

The night-duty shift of fourteen men lined up in a double line across the table-tennis room. The room also served as a parade-room. The local crimes and complaints were read out to us and Billy Budd posted each man to a beat. McLeod then strode in. He was a big, powerful man and he gave each constable a close scrutiny. He himself was immaculate but he reeked of drink.

'What-a-ye doin', laddie?'

'Learning beats, sir.'

'Who is he wee'th, sear-gent?' he said.

'Ransdon, sir,' replied Bill.

'Shue heem the groond whell, Ransdon, shue heem the groond ver' whell.'

He then turned to address the shift as a whole.

'Wee'th the exception of grub-time. I waant t'see noo man near the station until seex a.m.'

Bert and I left the station together. We struck up an instant rapport and swopped a little personal history. He had been a rear-gunner during the war and had been in the force for six years. Like me he lived local. Unlike me he enjoyed it. Bert on the other hand enjoyed most things. After an hour's slow stroll through numerous back streets, we reached the Old Kent Road. I was on my knees and there were still another seven hours to go!

'We'll walk back to the nick for tea,' said Bert.

'But I thought McLeod said . . . ?'

'Oh that's okay,' he chirruped, 'just as long as we book in for a WC.'

It was a mile-and-a-half back to the station. By the time we arrived there I was bursting. I went straight downstairs to the toilet. That night twelve men booked in for a 'WC'. I was the only one who actually went!

Our 'grub' period was scheduled from 1.30 a.m. to 2.15 a.m. We set up a card school in the canteen and when we returned to the streets three-quarters of an hour later, I had won four shillings, most of it from Bert. Now Bert was a lovely, amiable fellow in every way, but losing at cards was his real Achilles' heel. I could feel he resented it.

We reached the Old Kent Road again about 3.30 a.m. By then I was almost out on my feet.

'We'll stop this bloke,' said Bert, nodding in the direction of a tall fellow wearing a long overcoat and a cap. He was carrying a parcel under his arm.

'Mornin', guv',' greeted Bert cheerily. 'D'ye mind telling us what's in the parcel?'

'Don't see why I should,' snapped the overcoat. 'I'm going about my lawful business and you've got no right to stop me.'

I began to waken up. It looked like things were going to become interesting at last.

'Well I'm sorry, cock, but we *do* have the right,' Bert replied. He then went on to quote section 66 of the Metropolitan Police Act of 1839. This is an act peculiar to the Metropolis. It gives an officer the right to stop, search and detain anyone if he has reasonable grounds for supposing a crime has been committed. Bert considered that there was an element of suspicion in carrying a parcel near shops at 3.30 a.m. in the morning. His suspect on the other hand obviously disagreed.

After some minutes of arguing, Bert threatened to take him to the station to be searched. Only then did our suspect relent and agree to opening the package. It was all very trivial. His name was Clifford Harris, he lived nearby and he worked at Covent Garden market. He had left work early and he was taking home about 7 pounds of King Edward potatoes. He appeared to be in lawful possession of them and Bert was satisfied.

'Thanks very much, Mr Harris,' said Bert. 'Sorry you've been troubled.'

'Not so bloody fast,' retorted Harris. 'You've undone

my parcel, now you can do it up.'

'I'm not very good at parcels,' said Bert quietly.

'Then now's your big moment,' said Harris.

I could see that Bert was beginning to boil. He considered the whole situation was unnecessary. I agreed with him, although I couldn't help but admire Clifford Harris's nerve.

Bert suddenly grabbed the undone parcel from the pavement, slipped the string quickly over it and thrust the whole bundle under the right arm of the overcoat.

'Here's your potatoes. Now stuff 'em!' snapped Bert.

The string broke, the paper burst and seven pounds of best King Edward potatoes bounced cheerfully down the camber of the pavement and out into the Old Kent Road. Mr Harris was livid.

'I'll report you.' His voice rose an octave: 'I'll report you both. I've got your fucking numbers!' he screamed.

Bert turned to me: 'Come on or I'll pan this idiot. Then I'll have to nick him. I don't want to do that unless I have to, 'cos then I really will have to carry his bloody potatoes.'

We strolled on up the road. After a couple of minutes, I looked back. Mr Harris seemed on the verge of apoplexy. He was running into the road and, one by one, stamping on the potatoes as hard as he could.

'Look at them!' he yelled. 'Ruined! Ruined!'

'I don't believe that really happened,' I said to Bert some minutes later.

'Well it did,' he replied, 'I just wish I hadn't lost my temper. You should never let a bloke like that get up your back. I just hope that when he gets home, his house has been screwed and the lodger's raped his wife!'

This was my first experience of many incidents where members of the public were incensed at being stopped by the police. I have always found this difficult to understand. I have been stopped myself on a few occasions whilst off-duty, and have always found it a rather painless encounter. Unfortunately service regulations require a constable to obtain the person's name and address. This is allegedly to protect the officer from any future allegation. But this can often make a bad situation worse. Members of the public often think that this is adding insult to injury. Whilst many people are quite happy about being stopped, they are definitely unhappy at providing their name and address. I thought this a needless and undiplomatic regulation, because it caused far more trouble than it was worth.

The rest of that night was uneventful. I collided with Bert at regular intervals and soon we were greeted by the cheery 'Mornin'' of the early rising office cleaners. These ladies would begin to assemble at the all-night bus stops from about 3.30 a.m. onwards. They were drawn from all ages of the local population, from young mums to old grannies. Some were as tatty as tramps; some looked like Parisian mannequins. I never ceased to admire these ladies. Apart from the ungodly hour, they would walk through the most desolate of streets and alleys, invariably on their own. For my money they are the hardest working, happiest members of society I have ever had the privilege of meeting.

Bert and I emerged from East Street into Wharf Road at about ten minutes to six. It was a minute's walk into the station from that point.

'We're a bit early,' Bert said, looking up at the pawnshop clock. 'Come in here a minute.'

He led me into the deep gloomy doorway of the Dolcis shoe shop. He put his hand in his pocket and pulled out what appeared to be a small package. A thin grey light had begun to filter through the retreating night clouds though it scarcely penetrated into the cavern of the shop. He held the package out towards me.

'Cut!' he said.

I looked down and gradually made out the outline of a chequered pattern. He was offering me a pack of cards!

'But it's nearly five to six!' I exclaimed. 'I'm absolutely knackered, I can only just see you!'

'That's all right, just a quick game. You have got four bob of my money, you know,' he admonished.

I sighed.

'What're we playing?' I asked wearily.

'Pontoon.'

I had never received such good cards in my life. At one minute to six I was ten shillings up.

'Last game!' snapped Bert. 'Double or quit, okay?'

'Okay,' I groaned. I would have agreed to anything at that moment. I felt that I hadn't slept for a year.

I suppose his luck had to change some time. After 'buying' three cards from me, he showed me his hand. The five of hearts, the five of spades, the five of clubs, four of diamonds and two of clubs, a 'five-card-trick'! I was dealer, therefore I had an extreme outside chance. My first two cards appeared disastrous. Nine of hearts and seven of clubs – sixteen scored. I dealt myself another card, ace of diamonds; one more card, three of hearts. I was so tired I could hardly count. On the third attempt I realized that I had scored twenty. He, of course, had twenty-one.

'Last time,' I exclaimed as I heaved over the ace of clubs.

Another five-card-trick! But I was dealer – so I had won. I glanced up at Bert. At that particular moment he would have looked grey if it had been a July afternoon. At six in the morning, in a dark Dolcis doorway, on a cold March day, having lost a quid, he looked positively ashen!

'You jammy bastard,' he yelled. 'One last game!'

'Bert, it's one minute past six!'

'We'll play tonight then. Come on, quick, or McLeod will go mad.'

We raced over the road and into the station.

I cycled home through the side streets, not daring to venture on the main road in my exhausted state. I shed my clothes into an untidy pile at the side of the bed. The top half of me was slipping into the sheets before the bottom half had discarded trousers and socks. I attempted to answer my wife's 'How did it go?' but my words refused to make sense. I felt I would sleep for days.

I rose through layers of unconsciousness and lay staring at the theatre lights. The power of the glare almost burnt. A numbing sensation in my right arm gave me cause for concern. An amputation perhaps? What manner of surgery had I undergone? The drone of the bone-cutting saw merged with the 11.5 a.m. Morden to Cockfosters train. White cirrus clouds began to filter the power of the operating lights. The pins and needles in my right arm faded as, involuntarily, I slipped it from under my rib-cage.

Each of my senses eased grudgingly into use and I realized that I was facing the sun, through what appeared to be an uncurtained window. I turned to the brass-belled clock: half-past eleven! God, is that all? I thought I had slept for a year, and where are the curtains? I looked back at the window. I was now fully awake. The curtains were in fact in place, they simply hadn't been drawn.

I lay twisting and turning for over an hour. Suddenly I remembered a tip I once heard on the radio. 'When you cannot sleep, simply relax each part of your body in turn. First your feet, then your legs. When they are totally relaxed and limp and you have drained all thought of movement from them, begin on your torso. Then arms, fingers and finally head. Empty your mind of all thought and soon the tranquillity that you feel will pass into a deep sleep.'

I tried it, it doesn't work. You lie as still as a corpse but your mind is obsessed by sleep. The more determined you are to relax, the more your thoughts race. I did think that this could perhaps be a delayed action system, because on each occasion that I used it, by ten o'clock in the evening I could have slept like a squirrel.

Days and nights fuse for night-workers in a way that nine-to-five people can never understand. In the middle of winter, for example, it is possible not to see daylight at all until one's leave-day. Fortunately, the week had been a quiet one and my day-time slumbers had not been interrupted by court appearances. The weather had become very cold with powdery snow flurries. Crime, as usual, had fallen with the temperature.

4.   Out on My Own

The first parade after returning to day-duty following three weeks of nights was always a time of great confusion. We finished the night-shift at 6 a.m. on Monday morning and reported back for late turn at 1.45 p.m. the same day. Everyone found great difficulty in adjusting to the change of hours. Men rushed on to parade in various stages of undress. Buttons would be mis-fastened, socks would be odd and chins would bristle because of misplaced razors. The motivating force behind the first day of a quick change-over is simply to get the next eight hours over as quickly and quietly as possible. No policeman looks for drama when he is working sixteen out of the twenty-four hours. With any luck he can then climb into bed about midnight and sleep round to the following lunchtime.

We were inspected by McLeod who, although reeking of scotch, was again absolutely immaculate in his appearance. He stopped in front of me and looked me up and down, giving away nothing by his expression. He then told me that because of the manpower shortage and my local knowledge he had decided to cut my three-week period of learning beats to one week. Billy Budd then posted me to number twelve beat and a rush-hour traffic-point. He read out a few local items of crime news and at 2 p.m. exactly, the late-turn shift descended the station steps and spilled out on to the Wharf Road pavement. I was now out on my own.

I viewed the news with mixed feelings. Whilst I thought it would be good to be independent, I would miss the cocooning that I'd enjoyed whilst learning beats. It was therefore with no little apprehension that I walked at the regulation three miles per hour through the late-lunch shoppers.

I heard someone call my name and turned to see George Rearsden, strolling along a few yards behind me.

'D'yer know what to do at the Oval?' said George, referring to my traffic-point.

'No, not really,' I replied. 'Leastways, no one has mentioned it.'

'Well facilitate right-turning traffic and ignore pedestrians,' answered George, in a helpful tone.

'Ignore pedestrians?' I exclaimed, my head still full of training school idealism.

'If you don't,' began George patiently, 'the Oval will seize up in seconds and within minutes the traffic will have stretched down to Vauxhall, half-a-mile away.'

'So what are we there for?' I retaliated.

'You are there for about two hours. But if you start sodding about seeing pedestrians over the road, it will be more like three! Anyway, you'll find that out for yourself. Oh and by the way, if you want a cup of tea whilst you are there, go and see Arthur in the gents' toilet. It's not very good tea but at least it's wet and warm.' George stopped walking. 'I'll leave you here, I'm posted up the Old Kent Road. Good luck, son, see you later.'

He grinned, waved a casual arm and turned off into a side road, leaving me to my confused thoughts.

By the shortest route, twelve beat was about thirty minutes' walk from the station; but this being the first day on my own, I stuck rigidly to the main road. I cannot give any logical explanation for this, it just seemed more dramatic than the mundane maze of side streets. The route that I had chosen took me to the Oval in a semi-circular direction. It threaded its way past the only two big stores in the Wharf Road area – Woolworths and the Co-op.

When I had reached the front of the Co-op, I realized that a group of people were standing about outside Woolworths on the opposite side of the road. They were looking in my direction rather expectantly. I also noticed a large black saloon car. It was parked in front of the store, its engine running and the rear passenger door ominously open on the kerbside.

The training school dictum came instantly to mind: 'Remember, there is adventure around every corner.' Hadn't Sergeant McPhee repeated those words so many times? My God! He's right! I thought. My first few minutes on my own and I had obviously run into a drama. I looked back for George but there was no sign of him. Neither was there a sign of any of the other dozen or so policemen who had left the station with me, three minutes and two hundred yards ago. Why can you never find a copper when you want one?

I recognized the car as a Ford Pilot. That particular model was a status symbol of villains in the early fifties. A successful crook would announce his arrival amongst the big-time by acquiring such a car. It gave away more felons than a black face-mask and a bag marked 'Swag'. Nevertheless, if as a villain you wished to be respected by your colleagues, it was almost obligatory that a Ford Pilot was parked at your door.

Well there was nothing else for it, I'd have to go it alone. I felt in my truncheon pocket. I slipped my right hand through the smooth leather strap and my fingers closed over the fluted ends of the truncheon (or 'stick' as it was usually called). This actually presented me with an additional problem. I am hopelessly left-handed and police tailors do not cater for left-handed truncheon-carriers.

The bystanders looked quickly at me, then back to the kerb-side of the car. It's a robbery! I thought, and they are probably armed. I'll use the traffic for cover. I zigzagged my way across the road, escaping serious injury solely through the tolerance of a passing 35 bus-driver. I was vaguely aware of musical sounds mingling with the roar of the passing traffic. The front doors of Woolworths were open, and I assumed that the music came from their record counter, situated in the front of the shop.

At this point, I suddenly remembered seeing Bob Hope in a film called *Paleface*. He had to take on the local killer in a gun-duel and everyone gave him well-meaning but conflicting advice. Well I was determined that I would not get confused. I'd go straight for the driver. After all, if I immobilized the car and the driver, how could the bandits get away? Using the last few feet of cover provided by the bus, I ran round the front of the Pilot, with my truncheon partly extricated. At any moment I expected to see two crouching gun-men, emerging backwards from the open store. What I did see stopped me dead in my tracks. There was no driver! What sort of armed robber left their car unattended?

Suddenly, at the rear end of the car, I saw the cause of the crowd's interest. It was a one-legged harmonica player with a single crutch and a row of plastic medals pinned on the wrong side of his chest. He was performing a quite respectable tap-dance with his remaining foot to his own accompaniment of 'She'll be Coming Round the Mountain'. When he reached the part that I knew as 'She'll Be Wearing Army Bloomers . . .' he followed the crowd's gaze and saw me for the first time. At this point I noticed that a length of thick string ran from his wrist and disappeared into the top of his overcoat. Whether it was the sight of my truncheon emerging from my pocket or the determined look on my face, I'll never know. But suddenly, a second leg came swinging down from the long coat. He then snatched up his capful of coins and disappeared rapidly into Woolworths, trailing two yards of string from his left leg.

The crowd, many of whom had contributed coins, took the whole deception very well. Some shook their heads in disbelief, others simply laughed. No one seemed terribly upset. I guessed that our tap-dancer must have committed some sort of deception offence but I was much too bewildered to pursue either the offence or the offender. But what of the 'crooks'' car?

I looked at the vehicle for indications that it belonged to a latter-day Jesse James. A stocking-mask, perhaps, or a pick-axe handle? I saw a notice on the windscreen saying 'Doctor on Call'. Could this be a subterfuge? After a few minutes, Doctor Chambers, our police surgeon, emerged from the inside of Woolworths, carrying a large paper bag. The bag only partially obscured a rather gaudy, pink lamp-shade.

'Afternoon, young man,' he called cheerily.

He threw the bag and contents through the open rear door of the car and eased himself into the driving seat. Within seconds he was speeding smoothly away towards Camberwell. I left the main road, and as I headed towards twelve beat, I sought the sanctuary of the narrow alleys.

Some thirty minutes later, I emerged from the cramped streets into the pleasant open spaces of Kennington Park. The park is adjacent to the series of road junctions that make up the Oval. In those days, the ground, or 'manor' covered by Wharf Road Police Station, took in all of the area around the Oval, except the world famous cricket ground itself.

This was a bone of some contention between Kennington police and ourselves. On test match days, we had three men posted to the area – but purely for traffic purposes. One could spend the entire five days of a test match within shouting distance of the Oval and never see a ball bowled. Well, perhaps if Peter May or Dennis Compton were nearing a century, a call of nature might cause one to enter the ground to look for the lavatory.

With this in mind, I once walked into the rear of the stands during an England v. Pakistan match. My arrival coincided with a spell of very fast bowling from Frank Tyson. I must confess that I lingered a little on the way back. When I returned to my point some forty-five minutes later, I was a little worried to see that Sergeant Budd had chosen that particular time to pay me a supervisory visit.

'Where have you been?' demanded Bill.

'I've been for a slash, sarge,' I answered, rather unconvincingly.

'What!! A Slash!! For three-quarters-of-a-bloody-hour?' he exclaimed. 'You must have the bladder of a bloody camel! D'you know that I should stick you on a report for that? Still, now you mention it, I think I'll go m'self. Who's batting?'

'No one's batting for very long, sarge. "Typhoon" Tyson is bowling and wickets are falling all over the place,' I replied, in an effort to take his mind from my prolonged absence.

'Well let's just hope that he don't want a slash.'

On that sarcastic note, Bill turned sharply on his heels and strode off towards the Jack Hobbs Gates.

Although I lived just two minutes' walk from the Oval, I had never fully realized the amount of traffic that passed through its junctions. I began to feel very insecure. Was I supposed to control all those vehicles? After all, there was another fifty minutes to go before rush-hour really began. The volume of traffic would easily treble by then.

I suddenly remembered some advice given to me by Bert Ransden: 'If ever you get the Oval traffic-point,' said Bert, 'look in the police-box. There you'll find a white rubber traffic-coat. It's a bit on the large size, but don't do the point without it. You've got more of a "case" if someone runs you over.'

Well, there was the 'box'. We shared it with Kennington. It was just a few yards from the traffic-lights. This would be a new experience, I'd never been in a police-box before.

Throughout the force, these boxes were quite an institution. They were built of reinforced concrete, with very small, iron-framed, smoked-glass windows. The overall floor space was about four feet square. The whole structure would be about eight-feet high. They were, in fact, little more than concrete cupboards. Each box contained a heavy wooden shelf. This served as a writing-desk and took up at least half the total width of the box. They also contained a stool, a first-aid kit that was invariably incomplete, a partially empty fire-extinguisher – the carbon tetrachloride was unequalled for removing stains from police tunics – a telephone with a direct line to the local station, and about three thousand cigarette ends.

The box also had a flashing light on its roof. This was used whenever the station wished to contact a passing policeman. This light had a strange effect on members of the public. People who would 'look the other way' at a crime, or would cheerfully step over a poor soul whose life-blood was ebbing down the kerb-side drain, would literally go miles out of their way to find a policeman when the box-light flashed. Whether that policeman would thank them once he had been found is a different matter.

The box-phone was mainly used to 'make rings'. This was a system that was used to keep contact with men who were some distance from the station. Twice during a tour of duty a man would be expected to enter the box and report in to this station. A diary was kept on the shelf for this purpose. All ring-in times were scheduled in a small book carried by each policeman.

In spite of this long list of official uses, its main function was that of a haven. It was truly amazing how many policemen could squeeze into one police-box. The record, to my personal experience, is seven. Three standing, three on the shelf and one on the stool! All were wearing great-coats and most of them were smoking like chimneys. Smoke would billow out of the windows like Vesuvius before an eruption. On all of the occasions that I entered police-boxes, I never once saw a spider-web. It had nothing to do with hygiene but was simply that no living creature could stand the pollution.

I crossed the road, and with the key that was attached to my whistle-chain I opened the box door. As the fumes cleared, I could see two plump, middle-aged, pipe-smoking policemen from Kennington. One was sitting on the stool and the other on the shelf. They were playing cribbage.

'What'ya want, lad?' said the one on the shelf.

'Er, the traffic-coat, please,' I answered.

''Ere y'are then,' said the one on the stool, as he handed me the coat. 'Hop it, then, 'cos three-in-a-box looks bad.'

At that, the one on the shelf laughed uproariously. I, having missed the subtlety of the remark, closed the door with a weak, forced smile and walked slowly away.

I studied the white traffic-coat. Pale black may have been a better description. If the colour was dubious, the size was ridiculous. I tried the thing on and I honestly thought it was possible to walk about inside it. Even when I extended my fingers, I found it impossible to touch the cuffs of the sleeves. The shoulders drooped across my frame like a Dutch barn. The overall image was of the canopy that Post Office engineers use on man-hole covers. The weight of the thing was colossal. It was not only waterproof but, I suspect, bullet-proof too. One thing was sure: I was not going to wear that coat, neither on the traffic-point nor on any other occasion.

I didn't fancy returning to the police-box with the coat. I could just imagine the reaction of the two card-players. The one on the shelf would probably have a seizure. I was about to take the thing off and hang it on (or perhaps over) a lamp-post, when I saw the sign GENTLEMEN. Of course! Arthur! I'll leave it in his cubicle in the men's toilets. Not only that, George Rearsden claimed that Arthur was okay for a cup of tea. I gathered my skirts around me as I descended the staircase into the street lavatory. The coat swept each step in turn, as I eased my way down.

The cubicle door was open. I saw a small, red-faced, cheery little man, sitting in a double-cushioned chair. He was studying the racing page of the *Daily Express*. He looked up on my approach.

'Did you first 'ave that coat when you were a big fella, then?' he chirped.

I gave a polite smile.

'I'd like to take it off and leave it down here while I am working the traffic-point, if you don't mind,' I murmured.

'Sure, mate, providing we can find our way around it. Would you like a cuppa tea? I'm just making one for meself.'

'Yes, please. I've just got time, my point begins in a few minutes,' I said gratefully.

I entered the cubicle. It was spotlessly clean and extremely cosy. The room contained a small coke-fed stove. The kettle that was perched somewhat precariously on top of the hob was singing merrily. There was a table covered in some sort of washable material, with a knife, fork and spoon tidily laid. A threadbare but clean carpet

69

covered the floor. On the sill of the small window that looked out on to the wash-basins, a dozen pin-up magazines were tidily stacked. The only thing in the whole room which looked at all out of place was a notice behind the door. It read, 'I love a big negress in Red Silk Drawers.'

'Sit y'self down and take the weight off yer feet,' sang out Arthur. 'You can 'ang that tent up behind the door. Christ, it looks like the Albert Hall.' He chuckled away at his last remark.

I spent the next few minutes glancing down at the magazines. Young girls were posed in a variety of daring outfits that Mums today would go shopping in.

'Okay, here's yer tea,' Arthur said.

I looked up as Arthur slid the largest cup that I had ever seen in my life across the table-top towards me. Together with the notice, that cup was a contradiction of everything else in the room. There was hardly a half-inch of rim intact. It was chipped everywhere. The handle was missing and I could only assume that Arthur retained it because of its capacity – not for its elegance.

I looked around for another cup, in vain.

'Where's yours?' I queried.

'Don't you worry 'bout me, sunshine. I'll 'ave mine after you've finished. Take yer time.'

So saying, Arthur picked up a tall tin of abrasive powder and walked towards the six wash-basins, singing a few popular choruses from 'Annie Get Your Gun'.

George Rearsden was right. Arthur did make tea. He was also right when he said that it wasn't very good tea. Gruesome would not have been too strong a word for it. Throughout the street career of a policeman, it is a fair bet that he will drink more rotten cups of tea than will a member of any other occupation. Bad tea is a hazard of the job. The more militant trade unions would demand a bonus for even touching the stuff! The contents of that cup did not even look like tea. It was of a dubious, weak grey colour. It was sickly sweet. The amount of tea-leaves that floated on the surface indicated that the water had not fully boiled – yet the kettle continued to sing on the stove.

I did not wish to offend my benefactor so there was nothing else for it but to down the contents. Unfortunately, there was no sink in the cubicle. I lifted the tureen to my lips. After numerous great gulps, I swallowed the lukewarm ingredients without a pause. God, there must have been a pint of the stuff.

After a couple of minutes, Arthur returned. His musical repertoire was obviously wide; he negotiated the third verse of 'Danny Boy' reasonably well.

'Thanks, Arthur, that was very nice.'

He looked at the cup and stopped in mid-verse. The happy smile faded from his features.

"Ave you drunk the fucking lot?' he demanded.

'Why, er, yes, I suppose that I have. It was very enjoyable,' I bleated.

'Very enjoyable! Very enjoyable!' he repeated. 'You greedy bleedin' sod! 'Arf-a-that was mine!'

I closed my eyes in sympathy. Not so much with Arthur's loss but more with my own misfortune. I made some pathetic excuses and hastened up from the bowels of the pavement into the early evening rush-hour.

It dawned on me, as I took up my position on the traffic-island, that no one at the training school had given me as much as a minute's tuition in traffic control. I soon realized why. It is such a mundane, tedious, mind-blowing job that they obviously assumed that any fool could pick it up in seconds. I did make one big mistake though. I once stopped right-turning traffic to facilitate pedestrians. The resultant chaos took me twenty minutes to smooth out. My principles were therefore compromised on my first day out! So much for idealism.

I had spent an hour absorbing the lung-piercing fumes from the traffic, when I became aware that I was being closely watched by the attentive eyes of Sergeant Budd. He crossed from the pavement towards me.

'Where's your traffic-coat, lad? You'll get bloody killed in this light,' he roared.

'It's a bit big, sergeant, and I'm afraid I've left it in the gents' toilet, over there.' I pointed to the hole in the ground.

'You've never been in Arthur's Cabin, have you?' he demanded.

'I have, sarge, it's hanging up in his cubicle,' I admitted.

'Did he give you any of that "sump-oil" he calls "tea"?'

'Er, yes, about a pint of it as a matter of fact,' I stammered.

'More importantly – did you drink it?' persisted Bill.

'Yes. Shouldn't I have done?'

'Well, you'll shit for a week! Christ knows what he puts in it. I think it's a ruse to drum up customers for his bloody toilet. Was Emily in there?' queried Bill.

'Who's Emily, sergeant?' I asked.

'A big coal-black negress that he smuggles in from time to time,' explained Bill.

'Does she wear Red Silk Drawers, sarge?'

'How the bloody hell do I know if she wears red silk drawers!' he exploded. 'I'm beginning to get a bit worried about you. When you've finished here, make your way back to the station as quickly as possible. I shall have a job for you.'

By six-fifteen the volume of traffic had slackened visibly. Ten minutes later, the junction ran better when I ignored it. I took the hint and left my island. I began the long walk back to the station for my meal. I had not eaten since breakfast; I had rolled straight out of bed and into work, with nothing more than a cup of tea. My stomach had this vague feeling that my throat had been cut. As I passed by the endless little back-to-back houses, the smell of the evening meals tormented my eager nostrils.

I entered the station just after seven o'clock and ordered just about everything on the canteen menu. Sergeant Budd was wading through the most enormous bacon sandwich.

'You said you've got a job for me, sarge,' I said, dutifully.

'Never talk to me about work when I'm not at work, son,' he said quite pleasantly.

When my forty-five-minute break was finished, I entered the front office. Bill was in a customary pose, two fingers poised over the typewriter and his tongue protruding from the corner of his mouth. He looked up.

'What are you like with ghosts?' came the surprising question.

I'd heard about the many leg-pulls inflicted on new recruits. When I was in the army I had perpetrated a few myself. They usually work because the victim is so uncertain of himself. He would sooner risk the pitfalls of an obvious hoax than incur the displeasure of his new colleagues. He therefore takes the line of least resistance, even though, deep down, he suspects someone is trying to have him over.

'I've been told on at least three occasions, sergeant, that I'm very good with ghosts.' I hoped that this would call his bluff.

'Marvellous!' exclaimed Bill. 'Bloody marvellous! You're just the bloke we're looking for. Go up to 21 Nile Road; she's got a ghost. It calls nightly about nine o'clock. P'raps you can spirit it away, so to speak.'

'What sort of ghost is it, sarge?' I asked, hoping that my voice was not giving me away.

'I don't know, I've never seen it,' Bill answered thoughtfully. 'But I'll tell you what – it doesn't wear red silk drawers!'

I turned into Nile Road, a street of two-storey, terraced houses, let off into flats. There were three families in each house, all sharing the same toilet and bathroom. This did not apply to number twenty-one, however. Both ground- and first-floor flats were vacant. Mrs Katherine White lived on the top floor with her two children, a boy and girl aged four and five respectively.

I crashed at the knocker three times. The window of the top-floor front room opened and a tired, thin-faced woman of about thirty called down.

'Hullo! Who is it?'

'Police, luv. D'you send for me?'

'Oh yes. I suppose you've come again about the ghost.'

Soon I heard her faint footsteps descending the stairs. The door was then opened to reveal a tall, thin woman, wearing a straight, shapeless frock. The only other noticeable aspect of her was her hair, an intricate mass of curlers.

'Yes, it's nearly time for her walk, I suppose,' she said.

I followed her up the unlit stairs, past the two padlocked flats. She led me into her living-room. She closed the window and told me the same story that she had apparently told to several of my colleagues.

In 1941, at the height of the blitz, the flat had been occupied by an elderly lady and her middle-aged son. The son used to take shelter nightly in the garden dug-out, leaving the old girl to take her chance in bed. One night, soon after an air-raid had begun, the woman left her bed, possibly to go to the toilet. The time, according to the inquest, was 9 p.m. When her son returned upstairs in the morning, he found his mother dead. She had apparently fallen down the stairs and plunged sideways into the railings. Her head had broken a rail and passed through. Her feet had slipped on the steps; her neck was broken. She hung suspended until the following morning, when the police cut her down.

Periodically, she was alleged to walk the top landing, looking for her son. This would happen for several nights, always around nine o'clock. Then there would be no trace of her for several years. We were now in the fifth night of her walks.

I had already realized that this was no leg-pull. I sat there trying to make a nervous conversation with Katherine. She told me that she had landed from Ireland a few months ago. She easily obtained the tenancy of the flat simply because no one else wanted it. The amazing thing was that she did not appear nervous. The children were asleep. I was attempting to study the evening paper. Suddenly she said, 'Shsssssss!'

At first, I didn't hear a thing, although the fried meal I had eaten an hour before did a somersault in my stomach.

'I didn't hear anything,' I whispered.

'It's her, right enough,' said Katherine, softly.

I then heard a creak from a stairboard, then another, then a soft footfall on the rug that lay outside the door. I felt that I was shrinking in my clothes.

'Do – do you have a light on the stairs?' I asked, with a very dry mouth.

'No, bless you. There's no fitting.'

Suddenly, the door handle moved. It did not turn, it simply moved. Very clearly and very distinctly.

'She'll go now,' whispered Katherine, confidently.

I didn't really want to move away from my chair, but my uniform compelled me to. I rushed to the door and threw it wide open. The staircase and landing were completely black. I shone my torch along the landing and down the stairs. There was nothing to be seen. It just would not have been possible for any living creature to have moved from the proximity of that door in two seconds flat.

'Well, there's nothing here, luv,' I said, in what I knew was a hopeless attempt at a reassuring voice.

'There never is, she'll go now, at least until tomorrow night,' said Kate. 'All I'd like you to do is to tell the council about my situation. I'd like to get out of this place, a word from the police might help. I thought if a few of you policemen backed me up, I may get another flat,' she added.

'Sure I will,' I replied. 'Although I don't think we have much sway with the council.'

She led me down the staircase, then out into the comparative safety of the streets. I quickly made my way back to the station.

'Well,' said Bill, 'did you see the ghost?'

'I didn't actually see one,' I replied, 'but there is something almighty spooky going on up there, sergeant.'

'Rubbish! She's trying it on in an effort to get a new council flat. There's no such thing as ghosts.'

'I didn't think there was either, sarge. Now I'm not so sure,' I said worriedly.

'Well, tomorrow evening I'll give you another opportunity to make up your mind. By the end of the week, I reckon you'll be a pretty fair spiritualist.'

I cycled wearily home. I was too tired to eat and at half-past ten I collapsed into bed. Sleep, however, did not come easily. I lay listening as a distant church clock chimed away the half-hours. Some time around midnight, sleep began to infiltrate my confused thoughts. Ghostly harmonica players flitted in and out of right-turning traffic, although none wore Red Silk Drawers.

Suddenly I woke with a start. I'd left the traffic-coat in Arthur's Cabin. (Or was Arthur's Cabin in the traffic-coat?) Well, one thing was for sure – I was not going back to collect it.

5. Some Royal Occasions

I spent the next two evenings in Katherine White's sparse living-room. They were probably the most boring hours that I have spent anywhere. She could not, or more likely would not converse. It was quite apparent that neither the ghost nor I had been expected to return.

On Wednesday evening, I finally ambled back to the nick, where I was greeted by Billy Budd.

'How's your ghost, lad? Caught her yet?'

'A waste of time if you ask me, sergeant. That spook has definitely gone,' I replied.

'Well,' said Bill, 'I'm so pleased that you've shown this affinity with the dead, 'cos I've decided to spoil you. I've put you down for a funeral for next Sunday, and a very special funeral it is too. Queen Mary has died and we are going to St James's Park to make sure that everyone pays their proper respects. So wear your best uniform, a sad look and above all – don't be late!'

Sunday dawned into a very grey day indeed. I spent two long hours ironing, brushing and cleaning. I was so reluctant to take a chance on my trouser creases being damaged that I walked to work instead of cycling.

There were fifteen men from Wharf Road detailed for the funeral. We piled into the station van and soon we were deposited on the freshly asphalted surface of Horse Guards Parade. From our station to Westminster was just a short bus-ride over the Thames. In spite of this proximity, any reason that caused us to perform duty in that area was always referred to as an 'Up-town do'. This applied to all public-order functions, whether they were royal occasions, demonstrations or film premières.

After a short briefing, we found we were not to be employed on the funeral at all. We were in fact to form a 'reserve'. We were told to make ourselves as comfortable as possible in the potting sheds in St James's Park. Now with all due respect to the staff of that royal park, the potting sheds were not the most ideal or comfortable place in which a young recruit should be sitting about in his best uniform. We saw nothing of the funeral at all, although we could hear the massed bands playing suitably solemn music. Three hours later the ceremony was over and we were dismissed. We were left to make our own way back to our station.

This, then, was my introduction to royal occasions: the coronation, the jubilee, the weddings, the funerals, the state visits and the ceremonial drives. My personal view of royalty changed very much during these years. I had always been an anti-royalist but it truly amazed me to see just how much pleasure ordinary people obtained from the pomp and pageantry of the monarchy.

The first time that this was brought home to me was the occasion of the coronation of Queen Elizabeth II in 1953. Ninety-five per cent of the manpower of the Metropolitan Police was involved during the two days of the coronation. Some of the older officers, who were dug out of the courts, offices and stores, had not been on the streets for so long that they almost blinked at the light. The coronation was spread over two days because the majority of the crowds were in position the day before the crowning took place.

My contingent was on duty in Hyde Park in East Carriage Road. We had arrived there at 4 p.m. on the eve of the great day and we were to remain there until we were relieved by the day-duty, at 5 a.m. next morning. We took up our posts at the rear of the crowd and were spaced about thirty yards apart. There was already a thin line of police in front of the crowd. These were spaced at about ten-yard intervals on the kerbside. Each policeman usually carried a packet of sandwiches secreted about his uniform. Feeding arrangements in those days were quite primitive. A man had no means of knowing when, or indeed if, he would be fed.

We had been told at our station briefing that there would be a canteen somewhere in the park, near to Marble Arch. Later, several of my colleagues returned, stating that the queue for tea alone meant a forty-five-minute wait. Most of us decided not to bother. This decision was helped by the generosity of the crowd. They kept us liberally supplied with hot drinks, many of which were strongly laced with scotch or rum.

The weather was dry but overcast and considering that it was June, it was bitterly cold. The crowd, which was about eight deep and consisted of families and groups of friends, huddled together for warmth.

Our police capes were of a heavy glazed material, with a warm, thick, fleecy lining. Each policeman was clad in just his tunic and trousers, and shortly after nightfall men began to throw their capes around their shoulders in an effort to keep out the chill night air. I had already loaned my cape to the parents of twins, a young boy and girl aged about three years. They lay huddled together like the Babes in the Tower. Although they had indeed posed a heart-melting sight, my blood was rapidly approaching the texture of strawberry mousse. Walter Raleigh had received a knighthood for the loan of his cape. I felt I would be lucky to escape with pneumonia.

Just before midnight, the cold had penetrated me to such an extent that I had difficulty keeping still. The father of the twins, realizing my discomfort, reluctantly offered to return my cape. I declined, although at that moment I would have given a week's annual leave to feel its comforting rough texture around my shoulders.

'The cold doesn't bother me really,' I lied, taking yet another generous swig from his brandy-laden tea-flask.

Some thirty minutes later, I was approached by a tall military-looking gentleman wearing a white trench-coat and a dark bowler hat. He was accompanied by a slightly plump, attractive, dark-haired woman of about forty years.

'My wife's had a "turn",' he said curtly.

'What sort of a "turn"?' I queried.

'She fainted. She's still a bit groggy. Thought you might give her something. You know, a tonic? Something like that?'

I studied the woman. She was wearing a smart, expensive-looking, dark-brown suit, with a high-necked cream-coloured jumper and a single row of pearls. Her white face, in direct contrast to her black hair, indicated her recent mishap.

'How d'you feel now, luv?' I asked.

'I – I think it's just the cold,' she said weakly.

'I'm already feeling much better and – '

The husband interrupted, 'Look, I'll leave her to you. Must keep our place. It's right on the kerb, you know. She'll find her own way back.'

He nodded, as if in agreement with his own words, and without even another glance at the woman he stepped over the sleeping figures on the pavement and moved off towards Marble Arch.

I sought out Sergeant Budd who, after consulting a small pocket map, said he believed that there was a St John's ambulance tent somewhere in the park. He suggested that I accompany the woman in case she 'has another turn'. I was delighted – anything to get my circulation moving again.

Together, we left the crowd behind and set off across the grass into the interior of the park. I had no set plans, although I assumed the tent should be somewhere close. The night was pitch-black and the sounds were muted by the heavily leafed trees. There were no stars or moon, the only light coming from the now distant perimeter road and the equally distant gas-lamps that flickered by the Serpentine lake.

Conversation was stilted, until the first drops of rain began to fall.

'This is all we need,' I said cynically to my companion.

The occasional drops increased in volume until a steady downpour covered the park. We stopped under a large oak tree, not simply for shelter, for we also needed to take some bearings.

'Where exactly are we?' she asked.

'Well, all I really know,' I said, 'is that we are somewhere in the middle of Hyde Park, it's one in the morning, we don't have coats, it's perishing cold and pouring with rain. Do you think that if we eventually find the St John's tent they'll treat us for exposure?' I added.

She smiled for the first time and for about ten minutes we chatted. She told me her name was Margaret, she was an anglo-Indian and her husband had recently left the army after twenty-one years' service, mostly in India. He was in the process of looking for a new job. He had come to London for an interview, hence their presence in the park that evening.

There was no let-up from the rain. The first of the droplets had successfully filtered the leaves and they were falling haphazardly around us.

'What do you think that is?' she said, staring past me and out beyond the dark lake. My eyes followed her pointing arm. At first glance I thought I could see a ghost-ship with its great sails billowing in the powerful winds.

'It's a tent, or rather a marquee!' I exclaimed.

'What do you think it is for?' she queried.

'Dunno, it's too big to be a St John's tent. Let's try it; at the very least it will be a shelter. Can you run?'

Without waiting for a reply, I seized her arm and we scurried across the wet grass towards the sanctuary of the bulging canvas.

Our arrival, needless to say, was from the side opposite to the tent entrance. We circuited the canvas sides, breathlessly falling over unseen guy-ropes, until finally collapsing into the flap door. The storm lanterns that swung from the cross-poles illuminated a strange sight. Three rows of wooden tables and benches were lined up at one end of the marquee. Several figures were draped over these tables and a loud bubbling sound came from the other end of the tent.

'Are they dead?' said Margaret anxiously.

As I turned, I could see six more tables at right-angles to the others. These new trestles were absolutely groaning with food. There were rolls, buns, sandwiches, cakes and pies. A huge cauldron of water boiled cheerfully in the corner. It was a treasure-trove of goodies.

A woman in a blue nylon overall slowly lifted her head from a table.

'Are . . . are there many of you?' she murmured, through sleepy lips.

'No, just us,' I answered.

She groaned.

'We've been expecting hundreds and so far you are the only ones to turn up!'

'Do you mean to say, you've been here all night and we're your first customers?' I asked incredulously.

'That's right,' she nodded.

There were seven women and fourteen boy scouts in that tent and they had been waiting five hours to feed hundreds of hungry policemen. The same policemen, in fact, who were spending forty-five minutes queueing for a solitary cup of tea at the other end of the park.

The blanket-covered scouts lay fast asleep across the table-tops, like the long-dead slaves in a pharoah's tomb.

'D'you think we could have a cup of tea?' murmured Margaret.

'You can 'ave a bloody gallon if you like, dear,' said the lady in the overall.

After working our way through numerous sandwiches, cakes and cups of tea, a lull had descended on our hushed conversation. I was aware that the rain had eased. I looked at my watch; it read 2.45 a.m.

'Christ!' I yelled. 'I'll have to get back. My sergeant will be going mad!'

We thanked the lady in the blue overall and quietly made our way past the sleeping bodies and into the cold night air.

The grass was saturated, and the bottoms of my trouser legs began to soak up the surface moisture.

'Let's make for that path,' I said, gesturing to a footway some thirty yards distant.

'Isn't that a fence?' said Margaret, pointing to a wire-mesh obstruction between us and our chosen route.

'Yes, but it isn't very high, we can climb over easily,' I answered.

The fence appeared to be some sort of temporary structure and I negotiated it without difficulty. Margaret, on the other hand, was getting nowhere fast. She managed to get one foot on to the top of the post but could then go neither forward or back. I reached up to help her at the very moment she decided to jump. There was a clash of bodies, I was aware of a heel burying its way into my instep and my helmet rolled away down a gentle slope.

More important, I was also aware of her warm body. We stood for a second almost posed, with my arms around her and our faces practically touching.

'My son is about your age, you know,' she said softly as she slowly eased herself from my grasp. I felt about twelve years old.

We soon reached the comparative comfort of the path and within a few minutes we reached East Carriage Road. We walked slowly along the rear of the crowd looking for my colleagues and soon I saw the tall familiar figure of Billy Budd.

'Where the hell have you been?' he demanded.

'Looking for a first-aid tent for this lady, sergeant,' I stammered.

'What, for three bloody hours? What did she need, open-heart surgery?'

'I'll find my own way back now,' said Margaret, attempting to pour oil on troubled waters. 'You've been very kind and I've taken enough of your time. Thank you, sergeant.' She turned to me, 'And thank you, too, young man.'

She turned her face up to mine and quickly kissed my cheek. She smiled and strode quickly away through the crowds towards Marble Arch.

'Be kind to him, sergeant!' she called back.

'Kind to him!' exploded Bill. ''Ere, what've you been up to out there?' he added suspiciously.

'Unfortunately, not a lot, sergeant, but I found a tea-tent, if that's any help,' I replied.

Soon after dawn, the first of the early turn began to arrive. Our section was relieved at 5.15 a.m. and we were told to be back at our station by 3 p.m. that same day. We were to police a mammoth fireworks display at the Festival Hall near Waterloo station. As I walked home at five-thirty in the morning, across a bleak Westminster Bridge, I took stock of my situation. So far, my two royal occasions had been anything but royal. I had won five shillings and threepence on the first and a cuddle on the second. To date the House of Windsor was completely unaware of my existence. It was to remain so.

This, then, for policemen, is what royal occasions are all about. The actual ceremony or royal persons are only a very small part of a very large picture. The people, the atmosphere, the colour and the spectacle are really what make the day. I rarely performed duty on a state function that went according to plan. Well, not my plan, anyway.

Princess Margaret's wedding was a classic example of this. At that period of my police service, I spent most of my duty time driving cars. Therefore I rarely wore duty boots. I only had one pair and they were years old. They were cracked and creased beyond belief – but oh so comfortable! They looked the sort of boots that kittens should live in. On the morning of the wedding, two young boy scouts knocked on my door asking if they could do a bob-a-job for scout funds.

'You could clean my boots,' I responded. 'I'm going to Maggie's wedding and I'd better have clean boots.'

Well they set to work with a vigour, but although their hearts were in the right places, their polishing rags were not. They were arguably the worst-cleaned pair of boots ever seen on a royal function. The cracks and creases did nothing to help. Sergeant 'Phoebe' Fawcett, who inspected us that morning, took one look at them and said, 'You look as if you have been sitting on a small horse fighting tall pygmies armed with swords. They've carved bloody hell out of your boots.'

As a result of this admonishment, I was removed from the railings at the front of Buckingham Palace and relegated to attending to the security of the Welsh Guards mascot – a goat! This was a very well-groomed animal indeed, but a goat is a goat is a goat. In spite of this blow to my morale, I enjoyed the day more than my better-positioned colleagues. My lonely vigil with the goat obviously fetched out the maternal instinct in several young ladies from nearby offices. They spent the entire wedding period plying me with tea, coffee and cream cakes. The goat did quite well too.

Besides the improvement in feeding facilities, there has also been an enormous improvement in information services. It was never considered necessary to inform constables about anything relating to times of processions, who was likely to be in them, or even what route would be taken. It paid to study the newspapers carefully before going 'up-town', in order to deal satisfactorily with the public's eternal questions. One is constantly plied with queries on these occasions.

One of my colleagues, Doug Sorensen, devised his own system for assisting members of the public. He simply made up the answers. He gave the most hair-raising historical reasons for many of the ceremonies performed by the Queen. I would listen and marvel. Most of the time I would believe them myself. When the questioner walked away, usually well satisfied with the answer he had received, I would say to Doug:

'I didn't know that!'

'Neither did I. I've just made it up!'

One hot July morning found us on duty on the Victoria Memorial, just in front of Buckingham Palace. The occasion was a state visit by the Italian President. We had arrived, as usual, much too early and there was only a sprinkling of people along the Mall. An Italian family approached us and asked Doug which side of the Memorial the procession would pass.

'The left,' answered Doug confidently.

'How d'you know that?' I asked him.

'I don't. But it can only be left or right – can't it?'

I looked at the family as they took up their places on the left side of the island. They looked exactly like every Italian family that I ever saw in a Marx Brothers' movie. Both mum and dad looked as if they had been cast out of the same barrel. The six kids ranged between five years and twelve and their combined bums took up about five yards of London kerbstones. Momma delved constantly into a bottomless bag that seem to contain a never-ending supply of pastas and cheeses.

Eventually the Mall was jammed packed and the first strains of the massed bands' music could be heard coming up from Admiralty Arch. I began to feel extremely apprehensive. Doug, on the other hand, was engaged in a deep conversation with some tourists and was revealing a little-known catastrophe concerning the Victoria Memorial.

When the band reached the Memorial, to my horror it branched to the right. I saw eight eager Italian faces fall in dismay. I looked across to Doug but he was nowhere to be seen. He had vanished without trace into that thick crowd. I felt so guilty for him as I watched the Household Cavalry reach the turn-off. Suddenly I realized that the Cavalry were in fact turning left and the whole procession was following! Our Italians were delighted. I then saw Doug re-emerge from the crowd. He waved grandly to the Italians who all waved frantically back.

'You lucky bastard!' I mouthed across at him.

He winked and nodded agreement.

Many regiments and corps take turns in lining the royal route on these occasions. One of my particular favourites is the Rifle Brigade, or Green Jackets as they are now known. They are one of the fastest marching infantry units in the world; I can only marvel at their pace. On a State Opening of Parliament a few years ago, my station was on duty in Whitehall near the cenotaph. A platoon of these walking dynamos sped down from Trafalgar Square towards the Houses of Parliament. When they were parallel with the Cenotaph, one of the soldiers staggered and almost fell. He quickly regained his balance and carried on marching – leaving his beret lying in the middle of the road.

The squad came to a halt at the junction of Whitehall and Parliament Square. Each soldier was detailed to line a section of the route and they were spaced about fifteen yards apart. The hatless young rifleman turned right, stood at ease and stared up at Big Ben as if it was the most natural thing in the world. The roads were closed – the Queen was expected at any moment – but that soldier had the photographic attention of every camera-laden tourist in sight. It did cross my mind that he must have been bribed by Kodak. The clicks and flashes would not have been out of place at a world championship boxing match.

I decided to ease his embarrassment. Picking up his cap, I ambled my way in pursuit. Eventually I stood in front of the hatless warrior and tried to place the hat upon his head. Putting a hat upon someone else's head is no easy thing, it just never seems right. It is as difficult as tying another person's tie. I pulled his head to one side, I ruffled his immaculate hair. I almost removed his left eye, but at last the beret looked passably correct. I stepped back to admire my work when he uttered his first sound. Without any facial movement at all, he said:

'D'us a favour?'

'What?'

'Do up me bootlace.'

I looked down and there was the longest lace I have ever

seen, stretching away down Whitehall. It must have been all of four feet long, obviously the cause of his original stumble. The miracle was that he hadn't tripped up the whole bloody squad. I knelt down and hauled in the slack. Having finally secured the offending end in my right hand, I felt for the other end with my left hand. Search though I may, I could only find one end. I looked up at the rifleman.

'Where's the other end, mate?'

'S'only got one end,' he replied, again without moving his lips.

I accepted this statement for about four seconds – then the penny dropped.

'Wotcha mean, only got one end! How can a lace have only one end?' I snapped.

'All our boots 'ave laces wiv only one end, I tell you,' he hissed.

It was all too much for me. I wrapped the one-ended lace around his ankle so tightly that I feared his leg would fall off later. The last couple of inches I tucked into the top of his boot.

I eased myself wearily up from some street reminders, left by the Household Cavalry, and returned to my colleagues in the gutter. My pal on that occasion was PC Danny Cooke who had served with the Rifle Brigade for a time during the war.

'Where've you been?' Danny asked.

I looked at him for a second and replied, 'I know you are not going to believe this but do you know that Rifle Brigade bootlaces now only have one end?'

Danny stared back at me incredulously as the roar of the crowd told us that the Queen was about to pass by.

The rise in terrorism over the last decade has slightly changed the royal informality of the earlier years. Nowadays, prior to the arrival of the royal party, groups of serious-looking bowler-hatted gentlemen are seen to converse intently at strategic points along the royal route. On my last State Opening I saw one such group, standing on a traffic-refuge literally in the shadow of Big Ben. Their heads were together and each carried a very imposing briefcase. One of them would speak and the remainder would nod penguin-like, in unison. I could not help but be impressed as I stood watching from my neighbouring island some fifteen yards away.

About twenty minutes before the Queen's coach was due to arrive, a large black Rolls-Royce purred sedately down a traffic-free Whitehall and stopped by the very-important-people's island. A final round of head-nodding, then all of them except one piled into the car and it sped off into the Palace of Westminster. The person remaining, although not wearing the obligatory bowler, was clutching the equally obligatory briefcase.

The period preceding the arrival of a royal procession is always a strange time. There is an air of unreality – the roads have been closed and a strange tranquillity hangs over the streets. Even the crowd is usually quiet. There is an air of expectancy but nothing actually to cheer. One hears the child's eternal question, every thirty seconds: 'Is the Queen coming *now*, Mum?'

At this stage, the only movement on the street will be the Borough of Westminster roadsweeper. He will trundle his handcart to each scattered pile of dung left by the trotting horses. One such sweeper, all of four feet eleven inches in height, had obviously been allocated the section of Whitehall nearest me. He appeared to be either singing or talking to himself as he deftly scooped up shovelfuls of the rich droppings.

I was enviously staring at his barrow, thinking how its contents would give me the best roses in my street, when he spoke to me for the first time.

''E didn't oughta be there,' he said.

'Who didn't?' I asked.

''Im,' he replied, pointing at the remaining important-looking gentleman on the next island.

'Why not?' I queried.

''E's crackers, that's why not,' said the sweeper.

'How d'you know?'

'It's Nutty Sid, I've known 'im for years. 'E's as mad as an 'atter.'

I looked at 'Nutty Sid' with renewed interest. For the first time I noticed that his suit was quite grubby. On closer inspection, I saw that his shirt collar was badly frayed and dirty.

'Excuse me,' I said, 'but what exactly is your job here?'

'I've come to see the Queen,' explained Sid simply.

'Yes, but – well, do you work here?'

'No, I've told you, I've just come to see the Queen,' he repeated rather impatiently.

'What have you got in your briefcase?' I asked, slipping automatically into an officious manner.

'Documents,' he replied secretively.

'Can I see them?'

'If you must.'

He opened the case and tipped the contents on to the top of the barrow. Four old *Daily Mirrors* and a sweaty cheese sandwich fell on to the lid.

'Is that all?' I asked.

'Of course,' he said, in a superior tone.

'Well, you can't stop here, I'm afraid. You'll have to join the crowd on the pavement,' I said in more confident tones.

'Yes,' sighed Sid, 'I thought I might.' And picking up his 'documents' and his sandwiches, he slowly walked across the road and melted into the crowd.

'Told yer 'e was crackers, guvnor. I can spot 'em a mile

orf,' said the sweeper cheerfully.

A roar from the direction of Horse Guards Parade announced the impending arrival of the royal party.

I wondered how our 'suspect' had ever managed to join the earlier group. He had seemed harmless enough. I should think that the most outrageous act he might have committed would have been to offer the Queen a read of his paper and a bite of his sandwich. I put out of my mind the notion that the whole bowler-hatted group were equally crackers, even if they did enter the Houses of Parliament. I also wondered how long it would have been before they discovered Sid, had he remained on the island.

6. Bookies

The clock at St Mark's struck 5.30 a.m. as I pushed down hard on my cycle pedals. The wet flurries of sleet that gleefully followed the north wind had easily exploited the gap between my collar and my neck. I was not due to start work for another fifteen minutes and already I was soaked to my navel. A long, uncomfortable day stretched ahead.

I had pedalled furiously against the head-wind because the last man to arrive for early-turn beat duty usually received the traffic-point. I say 'usually' because sometimes he would have a valid excuse for being late or, worse still, for not being able to take up the point at all.

'Court at 10 a.m., sergeant!' was a statement guaranteed to begin the daily ritual of back-stabbing.

'I did the point yesterday, sergeant. There's some who haven't done it for weeks!'

Names would never be mentioned but betraying glances would make any verbal communication unnecessary.

Struggling with my greatcoat, I raced into the parade-room. I was surprised to see Sergeant Trucker preparing the daily postings. Arthur Trucker was not usually on our shift and he should have been late-turn that week. I whispered to Jim Irvine who had lined up alongside me:

'Where's Billy Budd?'

'Transferred,' answered Jim, without even opening his mouth.

'Transferred! Why?' I exclaimed.

'Some grief over bookies,' came back the numbing answer. Jim's lips remained immobile.

'What d'you mean, "grief"?' I persisted.

'Someone's been on the fiddle and Bill is taking the can back,' he hissed.

Men were still rushing on to parade when Trucker looked over at me.

'Who are you talking to, mate?' he asked.

'No one, sergeant,' I lied.

'Well, perhaps you'd like to talk to yourself for the rest of the morning, mate. Take up East Street traffic-point from seven-thirty until two o'clock.'

The laughter that came from the rest of the men was mainly of relief. It was always a good feeling when someone else received the traffic-point, especially when it was your turn.

There are many jobs in the police force that are really exciting, there are some that are totally rewarding. There are even those that are fascinatingly intriguing – and then there are traffic-points. To my mind, traffic-points are the best argument for not arming the police force. After an hour in the middle of the road, attempting to decipher signals from drivers that are often more difficult to crack than a Second World War invasion plan, I usually feel like shooting people.

At ten o'clock I was relieved for forty-five minutes by a young colleague and returned to the station for my breakfast. At eleven o'clock I was back in the middle of the road wondering how my mind was going to survive the next three tedious hours.

A few minutes after mid-day, I was surprised to see Jim Irvine walking slowly in my direction. He did not look happy. As a general rule, older policemen do not walk past traffic-points that are being manned by younger officers. This has nothing to do with any ancient force tradition. It is simply that his conscience will not permit him to. After all, it is a fair bet that the first copper to emerge within hailing distance of the point will be asked to take over whilst the pointsman has a quick fag, cup-a-tea or a 'slash'. The five minutes that are usually allocated for either, or all three of these functions do have a habit of stretching into half an hour, particularly if it is raining, and they are often a source of great friction. Therefore the older PC works on the basis that if he doesn't see the younger man craving for a smoke, dying of thirst or bursting for a piss he will not be tempted into giving way to his better instincts, i.e. take up the point. He will simply turn down any convenient side street or alley just before he reaches the unfortunate traffic man.

Of course the same rule does not apply if the roles are reversed (always assuming that an older copper would have been daft enough to get himself lumbered with the point in the first place). In that situation, every recruit would have been clearly told that it is the done thing to give the pointsman 'a blow' at least every half-hour.

Jim Irvine glowered at me.

'You've got to see the superintendent at half-past twelve. You ought to be back here by a quarter to one,' he said pointedly.

'Superintendent? Why? What for?' I asked worriedly.

'Not doing your bloody point, I should think,' he growled, as he slipped the white traffic-gauntlets over his arms.

Ten minutes later, I was standing in the corridor outside the superintendent's office. Having been kept there for the obligatory fifteen minutes, I was finally ushered in by his uniform clerk – big Jock O'Donald.

'PC Cole, sir,' said big Jock, reverently leading the way.

The superintendent looked up from his *Daily Express*.

'Ah yes! How long have you been with us, Cole?'

I could see my personal file on his desk; he knew bloody well how long I'd been here.

'Nearly three years, sir,' I answered warily.

'Three years, eh! Is it really as long as that? How time flies!'

He rose from his chair, placed his hands behind his back and walked over to the window. He gazed benevolently over his kingdom as it stretched away into the far distance, or at least as far as the Old Kent Road.

Suddenly he wheeled around and pointed at me dramatically. I was getting the full treatment today.

'What do you know about bookmakers, Cole?' he snapped.

'Not much. I've never put a bet on in my life,' I said puzzled.

'Do you know where all the pitches are on this ground?'

'Yes, sir.'

'Do you know any of the bookmakers or any of their touts and runners personally?'

'No, sir.'

'Are you aware of what has happened to Sergeant Budd?'

'No, sir.'

'Sergeant Budd was the victim of an allegation. I have no doubt, no doubt at all, that he is innocent. There is absolutely no evidence against him. However it is in everyone's interest that Sergeant Budd should be transferred. To avoid any repercussion of this situation, I have decided for the future to choose from a wider selection of men when I fetch out a team on street bookmaking duty. For three weeks from Monday next, you will be employed in plain clothes with Sergeant Hickett. Come back with him on Monday at 9 a.m. and I will brief you on what I expect of you both.'

He turned his back on me once more and resumed his

gaze into the distance. I wasn't sure what I was supposed to do now; he was really hamming it up. Why couldn't he just have sat at his desk like anybody else? Two long, silent minutes elapsed. I looked questioningly at Jock O'Donald. Jock replied by shrugging his shoulders and coughing lightly. The cough seemed to stir the superintendent into life. His body remained quite motionless but he turned his head slightly to the right and appeared to be addressing the cupboard in the corner of the room.

'Cut along. Cut along,' he said.

'Sor!' responded big Jock, and he led me back into the corridor.

I returned thoughtfully to my traffic-point, where to my mild delight I was in time to see Jim Irvine trying to disentangle the bumpers of a couple of delivery vans that had collided. His face was an absolute picture.

The following Monday I met Ken Hickett in the station canteen at about eight forty-five. Ken looked every inch a copper, his six feet seven inches causing him to stand out like an oil well in a paddy field, therefore I could not see us having a very successful month's hunting. He had a brief but eventful career as a policeman. He was one of the first products of the cadet-entry scheme. He became a sergeant about a year earlier than anyone else had previously achieved the rank, was an excellent thief-taker, a good rugby player and a superb fast-bowler. He was good-looking and popular with all. He appeared to have everything going for him. Everything, that is, except for his two weaknesses.

Ken's first weakness was his paperwork, how he hated paperwork! In those days, before the advent of the police administration units, sergeants would be responsible for the entire paperwork of their shift. Ken always worked on the ignore-it-and-it-will-go-away basis. At one time he picked up a great armful of correspondence relating to dangerous driving offences and tossed them all into the station boiler.

His second and greatest weakness was women, nurses in particular. He fell in love with a different nurse every week. The only time that I knew him to deviate from this romantic path was when he finally ran away with a Greek prostitute. This girl did not compare in looks with any other girl I had seen him with but she was a biological freak. Her periods only lasted thirty-six hours! On several occasions when I had called for him she would embrace him in a passionate farewell and say, 'Never mind, Kenee, tomorrow we will make much love!' In the two years that I knew Ken, I'm sure he lost height.

We were finally called into the superintendent's office. After tearing himself away from his window, his hour-long prologue basically boiled down to: 'Do not get into any unnecessary conversations with them, do not go into pubs with them and, above all, do not get conned into arresting "perchers".' 'Perchers' were always a problem. The main reason was that bookies and their staff were always a great deal smarter than the coppers who were trying to catch them. They had to be in order to survive.

The frequent changing of the personnel who were employed by street bookmakers was in theory a good idea. In practice, however, the rusc worked for something like twenty minutes. The first time either of the two men showed their faces on a pitch, their description – and any disguise that they may have adopted – was circulated around every other pitch on the manor quicker than tom-toms.

This constant changing also presented one big problem. It made the game very unequal. The degree of profession-alism reached by the average tout placed him in a different class to his adversaries – and it showed. Most pitches employed two men: the 'inside man', who would take the bets from the punters, and the 'outside man' who would keep a look-out for the law. The owner of the pitch would only rarely be in attendance. With sixteen pitches on the manor, the two coppers would only be able to make one visit during their three-week stint. Also, because of the limited time that the pitches operated, usually twelve noon till two o'clock, the two officers would only be able to operate in a small area.

Officially these men would work on foot. If they were fortunate enough to obtain the services of a vehicle, it would always be privately owned and never police transport. Even when an arrest was made, both the arresting officers and their prisoner would be expected to walk back to the station, or to use public transport. Many a prisoner has complained that not only had he been nicked unfairly – but he even had to pay his own bus fare!

Four of our pitches were little more than one-man businesses. The rest were owned by retired criminals who often found the housewife's shilling each way more renumerative than their former villainy. Many of these bookmakers would have full or part ownership in a pitch on other districts. They would also be into such dubious fields as unlicensed drinking clubs, second-hand car sites and scrap-metal dealings. Some of the pitches, however, were among the best established businesses in the area. These bookies would organize for their regular customers annual outings to the seaside, or a stately home.

The first problem that an inexperienced officer would have would be in failing to recognize that not only had he been 'sussed out' but that a 'percher' had been left for him. This was always some seemingly inoffensive little chap with no previous convictions. The words, 'Blimey, guv'nor, you really fooled me that time,' has convinced generations of young policemen that they have arrested a key underworld figure, just one step down from a Mafia godfather, when in reality the tout had been standing around for the best part of an hour, freezing cold, waiting to be nicked.

Most pitches were situated in seedy Victorian streets or alleys. They were usually in a basement or ground-floor flat with a convenient rear exit. There were occasional exemptions to this double-exit rule: perhaps the adjoining street would back on to the pitch so closely that there may not be room for a back entrance; or perhaps the property was more vulnerable from the back than from the front. Usually the tenant of the flat would be paid a few shillings rent by the bookmaker, although unless the police or someone who looked like the police appeared the flat would be hardly used. The business was always transacted at the door. In any case, some flats were infinitely more desirable than others.

One such basement flat, with no rear entrance, was situated in a quiet Walworth cul-de-sac. This den would be extremely safe from prying eyes. Residents and 'regular clients' only would be expected in Abbot's Close. Local folk-lore had it that Abbot's Close was built over a plague pit. If true, many of the victims must have been buried very close to the surface and still fomenting. The smell from the first basement flat was akin to month-dead crab-meat, it was so foul. Crabs were, however, a rarity in the Close. The aroma came most probably from the two middle-aged sisters who shared the tenancy of number nine. (Numbers one to eight had fallen down when the first German bombs exploded some fifteen years ago and about half a mile away.)

The pitch was owned by Ernie and worked by George, a slim and sensitive lad in his early twenties. George would always sit on the basement steps and take his bets. He was reluctant to move any closer to the front door than he had to. In his early days on the pitch, the sisters had tried to tempt him with tea but nothing would compel him to drink from their cups, so the generous offers had long ceased.

If the occasional stranger entered the alley, George would of necessity seek the sanctuary of number nine, but he would be careful not to close the door. At these times he would often feel faint through holding his breath. He had suggested to Ernie on numerous occasions that the quality of the pitch would be improved by a change of location. Ernie, of course, did not have to hold his breath, and the two shillings he paid the sisters was far less than he paid on any of his other four pitches. 'You'll be okay, George, they're nice girls, kindness itself they are,' Ernie would always answer.

One exceptionally warm June day found George very busy taking bets for the Derby. Instinct caused him to look up quickly as two strangers approached the pitch. He jumped the ten steps into the basement area and quickly slammed the door shut. He waited a full minute before breathing but eventually he had to give in. Taking a deep breath, he said to one of the sisters, 'Go upstairs and have a "butchers", Aggie, see if they are still about.' She nodded and immediately climbed the interior staircase. A few minutes later she returned.

'Still there, George, and they're watching the house.'

George was forced to take another breath in order to answer her: 'What –' gasp – 'What do they look like?'

'Coppers, George, coppers – and you should really do something about your asthma.'

A few minutes later Aggie again climbed the stairs; again came the same reply.

George weighed up all the facts. All the law had to do was to sit on the pitch for an hour or so. To miss an hour's takings on Derby Day would probably put Ernie in an early grave. Was it worth it? He was choking himself in that basement through holding his breath. If he wasn't careful either Aggie or Maisie would be making him a cup of tea to aid his recovery. George decided that enough was enough. Throwing open the door, he gulped the dusty street air and leapt the steps in bounds of twos and threes.

'Have a heart, guv'nor, it's Derby Day!' said George plaintively, as he imagined Ernie's reaction when he heard that he (George) had surrendered.

'Morning,' said the first stranger pleasantly.

'Morning,' echoed the second.

'Mornin'?' thought George, 'mornin'? These can't be coppers, they're too bloody polite.'

'Mornin',' he replied. 'Can I help you gentlemen?'

'We are from the borough surveyors' department and we are looking at the foundation of these houses; they look pretty rough, too.'

Propped against the wall behind them was all the paraphernalia of their calling.

'Christ,' thought George, 'all that bloody time in that stinking place, 'cos of two blokes from the town hall.'

'I'm sorry, I thought you were the law,' apologized George.

The two surveyors looked shocked. Then the taller one spoke.

'Not a bad guess, George, you're nicked!'

Treachery ! ! !

'Have you got a cold, George?' said the other inquiringly.

'No, but I'll probably have rigor mortis in the morning. Ernie will go crackers, nicked on Derby Day! He'll never forgive me, I know he won't.'

Like our 'borough surveyors', some policemen would go

to extreme lengths to disguise themselves in order to catch their prey. Ninety per cent of the time they would be recognized before they arrived within fifty yards of the pitch. They would wear decorators' overalls, postmen's uniforms, vicar's cassocks, false beards, real frocks and, in one case I knew of, a nun's habit. They would carry ladders, push ice-cream carts, ride in invalid chairs, lead donkeys, but almost always the touts were too good for them.

One of the few exceptions to this rule was a young policeman who was a fitness fanatic. Daily he ran the five miles from his home to the station in a red tracksuit and running shoes. His winding route took him past one of our most elusive pitches. After a couple of weeks the staff of the pitch became quite friendly. They would cheer him as he went by. Each day, though, his red tracksuit would inch nearer to the front door of the house. Each day, the security of the pitch lessened. Finally he pounced. Whether the £50 fine had been worth the two hundred miles he had run was arguable. I would personally rather have paid the fine.

Exactly on the stroke of eleven-thirty on my first morning on street bookmaking duty, Ken Hickett said, 'Let's have a pint.' Four words that made more impression on me than the hour of the superintendent's rhetoric. A few minutes later, we were the first customers of the morning in the saloon bar of the Duke of Sutherland.

After two or three pints and a cheese roll, I began to look anxiously at the clock behind the bar. If we were going to make the rounds of all of the pitches on our manor before one-thirty, we were cutting it fine to say the least.

'Don't you think we ought to make a move, Ken?' I said, pointing to the clock.

'Boozer clocks are always twenty minutes fast,' he

answered. 'Anyway, let's have another pint, I've got a plan.'

I try not to argue with anyone in a pub, particularly if they are paying. I waited patiently while Ken bought two more pints and kept his hand in by chatting up 'Big Jean' behind the bar.

'We are going to do this job properly, Harry,' he said as he lifted the jug to his lips.

'What job?' I asked, thinking perhaps he may have been talking about Big Jean (one could never be sure with Ken).

'This job on "bookies", of course,' he said impatiently.

'How? Let's be sensible, Ken, you are never ever going to look anything other than a copper, whether you wear a Salvation Army outfit or, or – a nurse's uniform,' I blurted out (I always became rash after a few pints).

Ignoring the obvious reference to his hobby, he said simply, 'On your bike.'

'Ken, I hate to tell you this but my bike is a five-geared drop-handlebar contraption that firstly I doubt if you could ride, and secondly, even if you did manage to ride, you will still look six feet seven inches. Your knees would be above the handlebars!'

'Not if you sat on the seat and I sat on the cross-bar,' retorted Ken, draining his glass. 'Your turn,' he added.

I took the empty glasses to the bar counter and wondered why Big Jean always got better looking when I'd had a few pints.

'Here's what we do,' explained Ken on my return. 'You ride your bike and I'll sit on the cross-bar. We'll swing quickly into the street and be on to them before they've realized what we are about.'

'But I've got a gear-change lever on my cross-bar.'

'Move it! Christ, it can't be that difficult, surely?' He was beginning to show some irritation.

'Where are we going to work this bloody miracle?' I asked.

'How about Tylers Alley? It's a sharp turn from the street but at least he doesn't stand in a basement. He's so bloody confident that he just stands at the door of the third house along. Unless he happens to be looking at the very moment we swing into the street, we've got him!'

It was pretty obvious that the plan was all cut and dried in his mind.

'Tell you what,' he added. 'We'll have just one more pint and we'll do it now, while we are in the mood.'

After four pints of bitter I am usually open to reasoned argument. Ten minutes later the gear lever from my cross-bar was lying in pieces on the floor of the cycle shed. No matter how we tried to move the wretched thing, it would not work satisfactorily from anywhere but the middle of the cross-bar. 'Take it off completely,' said Ken. 'It'll still work okay, you just won't be able to change gear, that's all.'

By this time it was almost twenty past one and time was running out fast. We pushed the bike in the direction of Tylers Alley and paused in the door of a baker's to rehearse our plan of campaign. With Ken on the cross-bar, I was supposed to build up sufficient speed to swing from the side road into the alley. The alley was only six feet wide so there was no kerb to negotiate. We would hurtle in, I would brake quickly, Ken would leap off and Fred Harris, that most elusive of bookmakers, would be at court next morning paying a hefty fine.

Every component of my cycle complained as Ken lowered his ample backside on to my cross-bar. Without gears to assist my pull away, the strain on my chain was immense; but nothing actually broke and we slowly moved away from the kerb. The road surface sloped down from the canal bridge behind us and this greatly eased my problem. The top speed we could ever achieve was at best a walking pace and slowly we rolled up the ramp of the kerbside that led into the entrance to Tylers Alley.

Fred Harris watched in total disbelief as two drunks on a bike swung precariously into his domain. We scattered numerous milk bottles and a black cat and suddenly I began to lose control of the steering as Ken's bulk restricted every turn I tried to make. I pulled desperately on my brakes but the little rubber blocks were fighting an unequal battle. Still Fred Harris stared in wonder. Then suddenly the penny dropped. He bolted into the door of number three and was just about to slam the door when my front wheel passed over the step. Ken, who by this time had incurable giggles, fell from the cross-bar and into the passageway. Fred surrendered immediately.

'You silly pair of bastards. You'll kill your bloody selves,' he yelled, 'and you're half pissed as well!'

Shaking his head in wonderment, he accompanied Ken back to the station. I had to carry my cycle on my shoulder because the front wheel was so badly buckled.

As we entered the station charge-room, Arthur Trucker was just finishing charging a shop-lifter.

'I've nicked these two for being drunk and disorderly, sergeant,' said Fred ruefully, as he turned his pockets out.

'Your evidence sounds more convincing than theirs, mate, but unfortunately you've got ninety quids' worth of betting slips – so you lose, sorry,' said Trucker.

Ken and I spent the next morning at court and the afternoon mending my bike.

'Sod that,' said Ken, nursing his grazed hands, 'I think tomorrow we'll be vicars. A bloke could get killed on your bike!'

I nodded a heavy head in agreement.

7. Tragedy

Death is not always tragic, of course. There are occasions when it is a blessed visitor, both to victim and relative alike. Most policemen, some time in their service, deliver a death message and are greeted with the words: 'Thank God! What a merciful release.' Other times, death can be neat and tidy and fit into place like the last elusive piece of a jigsaw.

Such an example of this was Mrs Dawson. I strolled along the Walworth Road one lovely spring afternoon and saw coming towards me a little old lady in a long frock, felt hat and carpet slippers. Clutching a Pools envelope, she stood patiently on the kerb waiting for a chance to cross the busy road. As I watched her, I saw her footsteps falter and her face rapidly drain of colour. I ran towards her and managed to grasp her by the shoulders just before she plunged into the busy road.

I sat on the kerbside holding her in my arms and knew she was dying. She was dead before the ambulance arrived. There were no relatives, no possessions and, as far as I could judge, very little pain. Her husband had died a month before, in their forty-ninth year of marriage. Two separate lives had met and fused together for close on half a century. One life had ended, the other, with seemingly no further purpose, had followed. The death scene could not have been more neatly portrayed in a 1930s MGM melodrama.

For policemen, then, death is a constant, yet inconsistent companion. Just when you think he is clean and tidy, as when he called on Mrs Dawson, he spreads someone else over the road like jam. He fools his victims and he fools us, the survivors. In fact he fools us most of all, because it is a certainty that he is going to have us over twice.

He fooled a colleague of mine in classical fashion. Bill was a policeman who really seemed to enjoy his life. He lived locally to the police station and in his off-duty time he worked unofficially in the corner grocer's shop. Policemen are not really allowed to do this – their service regulations strictly prevent any form of part-time employment – but Bill sailed serenely through that little problem for years. The only time when he had misgivings was when he took the tops of two fingers off on the bacon slicer; but that apart, life was carefree and good.

Bill was a slightly-built man who had joined the police at the outbreak of war as a 'war-reserve' and had remained in the force once hostilities were over. He was an extremely popular man who always seemed to be laughing. A bachelor aged about forty, he lived with his sister and brother-in-law in one of the better streets on our manor. I never heard anyone speak badly of Bill in the six years I knew him, neither did I know him to arrest anybody! I always felt that if he had not found his way into the force he would have made an ideal street bookmaker. He was in fact that station's bookmaker but that perhaps is another story.

Any local coach outing to a race-meeting would find Bill sitting in the rear seats of the coach, dealing the cards for two-pack rummy and puffing on his hand-made cigarettes. Here he was in his element. A couple of drinks would cause him to burst into song, his favourite being a song oddly entitled 'The Night the Dun Cow Burnt Down'. The Dun Cow, needless to say, was the local pub.

One lunchtime, Bill was on duty on a school-crossing. It was the crossing nearest to his home. This was always his favourite because he could spend most of the morning chatting to his neighbours. Suddenly a child darted into the road from behind him. A car screeched to a halt but not before the boy had received serious injuries. Now although the lad required a great deal of medical attention, it was believed that eventually he would make a complete recovery. Neither the driver of the car nor the parents of the child considered that any blame at all rested with Bill. Within days of the accident, the man who I had never seen without a smile on his face, gassed himself.

The station went into a state of shock, not at the actual death so much as the manner of it. Bill? Suicide? Never in a million years! The Bills of this world just do not commit suicide. Ah, but they do. In fact they seem to commit suicide more frequently than the dramatic neurotics who attempt it once a week and twice at Christmas. A station full of policemen, many of them with years of experience, who have seen life from every side and every angle – to a man they were fooled, as no doubt they will be again.

Christmas in the force abounds with tragedy. There are the deaths on the road: the happy laughing driver who is too drunk to see the singing pedestrian; the singing pedestrian who staggers into the path of the fast approaching car. These people we all know. The media and the public information services uselessly assail our senses with them every December day. All to no avail. Death is always something that happens to someone else, each of us is the living proof of that.

Yet there is a far greater cause of tragedy at Christmas, of which we rarely hear. There is no publicity, no statistics, just a complete indifference to its existence: it is loneliness. I rarely completed a Christmas duty without having to report a suicide, usually caused by loneliness.

197c Heygate Street was not the most desirable of bed-sits. In addition to the bed, it contained just the bare necessities: a rusty, milk-stained gas-ring, a small broken gas-fire and wall-to-wall squalor. To assist the occupant in his personal hygiene, there was a jug and water stand. The absence of cupboard space caused an assortment of clothing to decorate the picture-rail. The whole scene was completed by two filthy curtains on a sagging string. These rags obscured windows that had not known a clean for years. The only new fixture in the whole room was a length of red rubber gas-flex. This piping ran from the gas-ring into a huge plastic bag that lay on the bed. Also in the plastic bag was the room's occupant, a physically handicapped Kenyan and he was very dead.

Lying on a greasy chair alongside the bed was a three-page note. He was, it transpired, in love with a beautiful girl who worked in the same office. This young lady apparently oozed so much vitality that she looked like a commercial for milk. Although they worked together, she was completely unaware of his existence. The personal courage he had found to turn on the gas-taps, had failed him when it came to asking her out. Ironically the girl was so dishy that every man assumed that she must have been well spoken for. This wasn't, however, the case. Fed up with never being asked out, the fair maid had set sail for foreign parts – East Africa, in fact – hoping that there she would find a new life and some romance.

Poor Emil, unable to express his love, had watched her excitement mount as week by week her sailing date neared. Finally, she left the office for ever. The fact that she was travelling to the part of the world from whence he came, must have been the unkindest cut of all. Judging by his expression, his death had not been easy. A twisted little body with a twisted little face, in a cold, cheerless and filthy room, is not much of a mark to leave behind you.

I walked out of that flat a slightly different person to when I walked in. I had particularly wanted to be off-duty that Christmas morning, but so had several of my colleagues and I had lost the toss. My young daughter had reached an age at which Christmas was a time of magic wonder. I wanted so much to be there when she woke, to see those wide hazel eyes explore every package. If I wanted most to be at home with my daughter, where I wanted least to be was in this cold sordid room, dealing with a dead, crippled, idolizing dreamer who had been infatuated with an unobtainable woman. This was no way to spend Christmas morning.

Giving the body little more than a superficial glance, I picked up the faintly written sheets and began to read. For the first time that morning, my thoughts left the warm fireside of my living-room. The tree, the bells, the happy chatter of a cuddly, pink-jumpered three-year-old, all slipped from my mind as I read. I looked down at poor Emil; fate hadn't simply turned its back on him, it had kicked him in the teeth and ground its foot in his face.

'How about my bloody sheets!'

I looked around as the yell cut through my meditation. The landlady had entered the room. She was a deceptively pleasant-faced harridan with a voice like a rusty winch and breath like a long-dead curry.

'Have you seen the state of my sheets?' she demanded.

Emil had not died well. Just before he lost control of his senses, he had lost control of his bowels.

'Have you read his note?' I said curtly, handing her the flimsy pages.

'Yes, he must have been bloody mad. It was obvious that a girl like her would never have anything to do with a wretch like him.' I stared at her for a moment; the sadness in his lines had left her completely unmoved. It was Christmas morning, a man had died, and all she could talk about were her rotten sheets.

'They always complain when you ask for rent in advance, but now you can see why, can't you?' she asked as if seeking justification.

'I'll arrange for the coroner's officer to remove the body, but if I was you, I'd burn the sheets in the backyard,' I said.

'They'll be all right with a bit of bleach,' croaked the harridan. 'After all, you can't keep burning sheets every time you have a new lodger, can you?'

'Oh! Do all of your lodgers commit suicide then?' I asked, with about as much sarcasm as I could muster. 'Perhaps you should ask them to throw themselves under a train. It would be a lot easier on your bed-linen.'

She looked at me for a moment, then she said in a surprisingly soft voice: 'You are right. I am making a fuss. After all, it is Christmas. Would you like a drink?'

'No thanks.' I just wanted to get out in the air. 'I'll take possession of the letter for the coroner and I'll see you at the inquest. Happy Christmas.'

I walked back to the station and I could think of nothing else but the hopelessness that Emil must have felt when he finally turned on the gas. Two days into the New Year, the coroner decided that Emil had 'Taken his life whilst the balance of his mind was disturbed'. I would have thought that on that Christmas morning, probably for the first time in years, if not in his whole life, Emil knew exactly what he wanted and he had reached out and taken it.

Not all tragedy manifests itself in death, of course. The large door that led to the inquiry counter of Wharf Road station creaked slowly open one spring day and a scrawny, dirty-looking woman aged about sixty shuffled up to the counter. I thought at first glance that she was accompanied by a dog on a lead but I could not actually see the animal over the waist-high counter. Her left arm was held down, close to her side, while her right arm gesticulated wildly as she recited her story.

It appeared that her twenty-year-old single daughter had given birth to a half-caste boy some three years previously. The girl had been in the habit of sleeping around and had never been really sure of the identity of the father. She subsequently gave as much thought to the child as she had given to her own life and soon left home to live with a sailor from Hull. The child was therefore left in the care of the grandmother. Unfortunately the woman at the counter was neither 'grand' nor 'motherly'.

As I moved closer to the counter to listen to the story, I was aware that the 'dog' was in fact a small half-caste mongol girl aged about three. I instantly assumed that the daughter had been sleeping around even more than Mum had perhaps at first realized. The child clung tightly to the woman's filthy hand and gazed adoringly up at her face. The look of pure trust in her eyes strangely moved me.

'So what am I gonna do to get some more money? It's all right for her, she's pissed off with the sailor and left me with the sodding kid. I reckon I'm entitled to a few quid every week. Stands to reason, I'm feeding the kid and I fink I oughta get paid for it,' said the old lady, concluding her story.

Now while I appreciated the financial difficulty that she must have found herself in, not once during her conversation did affection, love or concern for the child show through. Always it was money.

'Wait a minute!' I snapped impatiently, picking up pen and paper. 'Give me some details. Is this another child?' I pointed at the small girl.

'Nah! It's 'im,' she said.

'What d'you mean "him", it's a girl, isn't it?' I exclaimed in puzzlement.

'Can't you tell the sodding diference between a boy and a girl? Christ! No wonder there are so many sodding murders!'

It was not until that moment that the truth struck me. The illegitimate grandson was here at the counter, dressed in a filthy frock that was three inches too long! I looked again at the child; again adoration beamed up at the crone.

'Why have you dressed him in girl's clothing, then?' I asked.

'It's all I've sodding got! They were some old clothes that belonged to me daughter. Anyway, what difference does it make what he wears? He's a mongol and too silly to know any better.'

I froze in pity. I called over to the station officer.

'There's a lady with a complicated social problem, sarge, perhaps you'd better deal with it.'

I did not even wait for a reply but dashed out of the office and stood on top of the steps that led down into the station yard. I felt as if someone had removed the king-pin from my brain. My thoughts and emotions flew around in a confused whirl refusing to settle on any logical foundation. I wanted to rush back into the front office and snatch up the boy and scream at the woman: 'You can't have him, you wicked old bitch.' I wanted to take him home, dress him in shirts and trousers, play rough-and-tumble games on the living-room carpet. I wanted to buy him football boots, a train set and toy motor cars. Yet in spite of these feelings, all I really did was stand there and feel totally inadequate. I wouldn't take him home, of course. I could not solve every single emotional problem by picking it up and taking it with me. Yet I knew that when I finally went home, there was no conceivable way that I was going to remove that child from my mind.

The station officer had obviously given her the benefit of his greater knowledge and I saw the pair of them walk out into the street. As I watched them melt into the crowds of shoppers, the child's gaze never once left the woman's face. I walked back into the front office and I wondered how the incident had affected the station officer.

'Isn't it about time you made some tea, then?' he said, as he resumed his typing.

Being the bearer of bad news, whether it is a death or a serious accident, is probably one of the most unpleasant tasks that any policeman faces. How can you tell a person that a loved one has died? There is no magic formula. I have known many men who would use any excuse to get out of the task. Some will just blurt out the news and almost run, not because they are unsympathetic but simply because they are afraid of their own emotions. There is a story in police folk-lore that I do not believe for a moment concerning such a message, and every old copper that I ever met assured me that he knew the PC in question. Whether the tale has some basis in fact I do not know but it does bear out a point.

A woman was to be informed that her husband had been suddenly killed in an accident at work. The officer knocked on the door and is alleged to have asked if widow Brown lived there. 'No, just me, Mrs Brown,' came back the puzzled reply. 'That's what you think, luv,' he answered and he walked briskly away. I have no doubt that that conversation never actually took place, certainly not with those exact words, but there must have been times when the dialogue became perilously similar.

I received a message early one afternoon, to tell a Mrs Jean Rogers of 27b Pullens Buildings that her husband had been killed that morning in a crash. It had happened just after he had crossed on the Channel ferry to Calais. The impact had been so great that he was completely unrecognizable and the French police had only been able to identify him from his driving licence.

Pullens Buildings drove a bus through every sociological theory concerning environment. The buildings were crowded, four-storey Edwardian tenements. They had no bathrooms, the plumbing was a joke and the stone staircases were death traps. They were situated across five streets of our manor and they were absolutely immaculate. They were never vandalized, trouble between neighbours was almost non-existent and they had a community spirit second to none. They were usually referred to simply as 'Pullens' and they were absolutely unique.

As I climbed the spotlessly clean steps that led to the third floor, I wondered how old Mrs Rogers would be. I always dreaded telling an older person bad news, so much more than a younger one. The hysteria that was almost obligatory from the old was strangely absent from the young. The door opened in answer to my knock and revealed a pretty young girl, of about twenty-two, clutching a freshly bathed baby to her shoulder.

'Morning,' she smiled.

This in itself was unusual. Most people always anticipate bad news when a policeman calls. Obviously tragedy was never in this girl's mind.

'Mrs Rogers?' I asked.

'Yes.'

'Is your husband George Arthur Rogers?'

'Well, yes, he is,' she said, looking puzzled. Still no trace of anxiety showed in her face.

'Can I come in, luv? I want to talk to you,' I said.

'Sure, sit yourself down anywhere.'

She led me into a comfortably furnished living-room. I

sat on the settee and she sat opposite me on an armchair and resumed dressing the baby.

'Is your husband a lorry-driver, Mrs Rogers?'

'Yes.'

'Well I'm very sorry but he was killed in a car smash this morning.' I paused to let the words sink in. 'Can I tell any of your neighbours or friends? Perhaps you'd like them here?' I suggested.

'I don't believe it,' she said, suddenly looking pale. 'When did it happen?'

'About four hours ago. Apparently he hit another vehicle head-on,' I answered.

'I just know that it is not true,' she said softly. I noticed that she was clutching the baby much more tightly.

'Can I make you a cup of tea or something?' I offered, desperately trying to be of use.

'But when he left here this morning, he said he wouldn't be late. He said he might even be home early today. He just can't be dead, I know he can't.'

'Well I'm sorry, luv, but I'm afraid he – what time did he leave this morning for work?' I suddenly asked, not really knowing why.

'Eight o'clock,' she whispered.

'Well he couldn't have hung about much, he was in Calais at ten!'

'Calais!!' she exclaimed.

'Yes.'

'What, Calais in France?'

'Of course.'

'But he only works in Wapping and he never goes out of London!' she almost yelled.

'Well he was so badly injured that he could only be recognized by his driving licence,' I explained.

'But he lost his licence in a break-in some weeks ago.' Her voice had risen dramatically. The thought hit us both at the same time. George Arthur Rogers was safe and well and working in Wapping. The crook who broke into his flat a few weeks previously was now being scraped from the driving cabin of a lorry in northern France!

'God! I'm so sorry, Mrs Rogers, but – '

'That's okay, that's fine!' she interrupted. 'You've given me my husband back!'

'You'd better make a bloody great fuss of him when he comes home,' I suggested.

'Oh I will! I will!' she exclaimed.

I walked down the steps and out into the street. It was a blessing that she was so young. The shock could have killed an older person. I wondered just who it was who was dead in Calais. One thing was for sure, George Arthur Rogers was going to have one marvellous evening when he arrived home later that day.

8. Murder Most Foul

As a general rule, it used to be possible for a uniformed policeman to serve his entire twenty-five or thirty years' service without as much as a sniff of a murder. At least that *was* the case until a few years ago. The chances of a murder today, however, have increased dramatically. Until the mid-1960s, there had only been one murder on the Wharf Road manor in twenty-five years. It must be said in fairness that during that period there had been several near misses and not a few of our local 'heavies' had been involved in murders elsewhere. (The Richardson gang were nearly all locals and the Krays also enrolled staff from south-east London.) Nevertheless, our own manor was fairly clear of the capital offenders.

During the sixties, violence began to escalate sharply. I first noticed this tendency in the disturbances that we were called to in public houses and drinking-clubs. In the fifties there would be the Saturday night fights, which would usually result in black eyes and similar facial abrasions. Within a year or two, the injuries became deep lacerations, caused by broken bottles, stilettos or reinforced toe-caps. I know no obvious reason for this, other than the fact that society as a whole seemed far more ready to accept violence than it had ever been before.

This was first noticeable in the school-playground fights. Boys have always fought in the playgrounds but the battle used to end when one lad was knocked to the floor. The other would be regarded by all as the victor and that usually would be the end of the matter. Unfortunately we reached a stage when the fight had hardly begun when one boy did in fact hit the floor. This would be a green light, not only for his assailant but anyone else who felt so inclined, to rush in and give him a kicking.

The elderly, in particular, reacted to this escalation in violence by making themselves more insular. They fitted extra locks on their doors and built cosy little worlds inside their houses. There was little that would cause them to venture out after dark. Witnesses were harder to find and the golden rule became 'Don't get involved'. Victims of crime were ignored, and it became only a small step to the stage where murder became comparatively acceptable. One Wharf Road killing at this time was committed by a seventeen-year-old boy who chased another lad two hundred yards to plunge a knife into his neck. At the Old Bailey some months later he was sentenced to three years' probation and one hell of a telling off.

The one murder that we did have in those early years had nothing to do with any of society's changing attitudes. It was a fairly straightforward murder in which the suspect was known almost as soon as the body was discovered. It was caused more by the perpetrator's mental state than his environment. It could have happened in any age or any time; all it needed was the players, and we always seemed to have the players at Wharf Road.

Two colleagues of mine, Max Evans and Jock Kinsella, had been called by neighbours to 168 The Albany, a fourth-floor tenement flat. The Albany was about six storeys high and each individual block entrance led to the usual smooth-stone staircase. The Albany was slightly different to most tenement blocks inasmuch as the staircase was spiral. There was an iron grille lying across the well of the staircase on each floor level. This was designed to stop young children and old drunks plummeting down the stair-well.

The occupant of 168 had not been seen for several days. He was described as middle-aged, scruffy and not very bright. Max knocked loudly on the door for some minutes but received no reply. The front door was very substantial and the letter-box had a heavy backing of cloth that blocked any vision beyond it. If The Albany front doors had one weak spot, then it was the fan-light. These were usually pieces of fabric-covered glass that measured about two feet by one-and-a-half feet and they were situated immediately above the doors.

Jock Kinsella grabbed Max around his thighs and bodily lifted him three feet off the floor. Max scratched frantically at the front of the glass but made little impression on the waxed fabric. Jock soon tired of his burden and with a grunt let Max slip down into a standing position. They had been no more successful with the fan-light than they had been with the letter-box. After a brief consultation, they decided to break the fan-light. They were influenced in arriving at this decision by the smell that was filtering through the door frame. It was a cold, damp, misty November evening but the smell gave a fair indication of what lay inside the flat.

Again Max was raised towards the fan-light and this time, after a couple of hefty whacks with his truncheon, the glass shattered. The silence that followed the crashing of the glass seemed almost oppressive.

'Are you there, Mr Roberts?' called Max, who by this time had his left foot on the door-handle and his head through the broken fan-light.

'What can you see?' demanded Jock impatiently.

'Nothing for the moment, it's pitch black – Christ!!! There's blood everywhere!'

Lying immediately behind the door, and only just

discernible from the dim staircase light, was a body. Just whose body it was, Max could not make out.

'Let me have your torch for a moment, Jock,' he called down.

'Sorry, but I haven't got it with me, it's broken,' apologized Jock.

Two policemen on a dark November evening with a mutilated body and not a light between them! This may seem surprising, yet it was in fact quite normal at that period, because of the appalling standard of the torches that had been issued throughout the Metropolitan Police. They had been specially designed to fit into a small oblong pocket in our raincoats. Fit they did   light they wouldn't. The few that did light would not turn off! To add interest, if they were not used for a week they would corrode in a most amazing fashion. If they were not used for two weeks, they took on the appearance of cauliflowers.

Knocking out the remainder of the glass, Max decided that he would try to drop down into the narrow passageway. It was no easy task to squeeze through such a small gap but, having accomplished it, he easily leaped over the body that lay slumped against the inside of the door. He reached out and slid back the bolt that secured the door. Suddenly Jock called sharply from outside the door:

'Where's the body?'

'Against the door. Incidentally it's a woman – or it was!' said Max.

'Well then don't open it, at least until the DI [detective inspector] has been here. Look, I'll run back to the station and get some assistance, but whatever you do TOUCH NOTHING or the DI will have your guts for garters,' ordered Jock.

'What am I supposed to do, then?' queried Max anxiously.

'Make yourself comfortable somewhere, I'll be as quick as I can.'

Jock was already running down the stairs before the last of his words had reached Max's ears. As the last of Jock's footsteps faded away, Max decided to explore the flat. By this time his eyes had adjusted slightly more to the dark and sufficient light filtered up from the street lamps for him just to make out a window and shadowy pieces of furniture. He groped around the room until he found the end of a settee. He lowered himself into the corner of it and thought that it may be just as well that he could not actually see the room. The smell told him that it was anything but clean and he was fairly sure that if he had been able to see the furniture clearly, he would never wish to sit on it.

Max fumbled in his tunic pocket until he found his tin of tobacco and cigarette papers. Certainly up until the sixties, most policemen would no more walk the streets without their tobacco tin than they would without their trousers. He placed a small quantity of tobacco in the frail paper and began to roll. With the cigarette held parallel to his lips and his tongue protruding in the act of licking, he had a sudden thought. He was four floors up, the door was bolted from the inside and the body was chopped up against the locked door. It was fairly safe to assume that it wasn't suicide. Therefore unless the attacker had either leaped sixty feet out into the chill evening air, he was still in the flat! But where?

'Have you come for me?' said a faltering voice somewhere close at hand.

Max searched desperately for his temperamental lighter. Click – click – click, finally the lighter sparked reluctantly into life. The shadows in the room danced briefly to the irregular rhythm set by the flickering flame. Max soon realized that the movement of the shadows was prolonged more by his trembling hand than any inconsistency in the flame. One shadow that was ominously close, the other end of the settee in fact, was talking to him:

'She was a dirty woman you know, I had to hit her – she was wicked.'

Max raised the lighter slightly to obtain a clear view. Sitting three feet away from him was a wild-eyed, bearded figure nursing a blood-stained axe!

'Would you – would you, like a cigarette?' said Max hoarsely, offering the figure his tin.

'No, thank you. I don't smoke. I think it is wicked to smoke,' said the voice, becoming slightly more aggressive.

'So do I,' said Max, hastily returning the tobacco tin to his pocket.

'She was very wicked, you know,' said the man, his voice rising higher at every word.

'I'm sure she was, I'm sure she was,' replied Max soothingly.

During the next ten minutes, which were also the longest of his life, Max made more banal small talk than he had ever accomplished before. He agreed with everything the man suggested but never once did he take his eyes from either him or his axe. Max said later that he considered diving for the weapon on several occasions but if he failed to secure it, what then? That one thought made him talk as never before and, being Welsh, he could talk a fair bit at the best of times.

Eventually, Jock Kinsella and several CID officers arrived. The door was taken from its hinges and removed outwards. Mr Roberts was led down the passageway and stepped over the body with no sign of recognition. It was all very simple and straightforward. She had been a prostitute whom he had picked up at Waterloo. He had taken her to his flat and eventually killed her with the axe.

He was obviously insane and he complied quietly with every request made to him. When taking down his statement, the DI asked him what he did after he killed the woman.

'I cut my throat,' he said

'You what?' exclaimed the DI.

'I cut my throat, see – ' so saying, he lifted back his head and there beneath the black beard was a wide gash across the whole width of the throat. He had been sitting in that flat with his throat cut for several days. He had originally passed out through loss of blood but when his head slumped forward the wound had closed and the flow of blood was greatly reduced or even stopped altogether. He had so many blood-stains on him that no one had noticed his throat. He was eventually certified insane and later committed to an asylum. Max always used to say that he had his doubts about just how insane Mr Roberts actually was.

'After all,' he claimed, 'he didn't kill her until he'd had his "wicked way" with her, so he couldn't have been that crackers could he?'

'Perhaps she nagged,' Jock would suggest.

One problem when dealing with any incident for the first time is that it is very easy to make mistakes. If a member of the public calls a policeman, whatever the incident, he always expects him to know all about the subject, whether it is dog distemper or high treason. Experience in any field must give a person a certain amount of panache – if not necessarily in the subject at hand, then at least in the ability to convince the public that you know what the hell you are talking about, even when you haven't a clue. Occasionally, of course, it all goes wrong and when it does, oh boy, how your colleagues let you know.

The 'eternal triangle' has been responsible for so many

murders that when one reads that a senior detective is leaving the force and that during his service he has solved twenty or so murders, it would be interesting to know exactly how many of them were affairs of the heart. Most of these could usually be solved by a small boy and his dog.

On a hot summer day recently, an irate husband traced his wife and her lover to their love-nest on the fourth floor of a block of council flats. His revenge was swift, brutal and merciless. He stabbed the man to death and then chased the wife down the stairs, finally catching up with her at ground level. He meted out the same fate to her and then fled. The doors that had been shut in her face whilst she had been running for her life slowly opened. The first brave soul approached the woman and saw, quite rightly, that both police and ambulance were needed. The ambulance arrived first on the scene and the crew immediately realized the man was beyond all earthly help. They then concentrated all their efforts on the dying woman. She, poor girl, breathed her last just as the police car screeched to a halt. Dick Smith had never been called to a murder before, and the radio message – 'Man berserk with a knife' – caused him to wonder apprehensively just what he would find at the scene.

Dick led the two other crew members of police car 'Mike 3' as they ran across the forecourt to the spot where the ambulance crew were bending over the dead girl.

'There's another one upstairs on the top floor, mate,' said the ambulance driver, 'and he's dead on the bed.'

Dick did not wait for the lift but rushed up the stairs two and three at a time. He arrived breathlessly at the top landing and ran into an open door. The bedroom was directly in front of the flat entrance and Dick could immediately see the body spread-eagled on top of the bed, the eyes closed and the mouth open.

Part of Dick's training caught up with him at that

moment: 'Don't let any bloody oaf clump all over the scene of a crime,' was the basic theme of it. He called back to his two colleagues: 'He's in here and he's well dead. Keep everyone else out.' So saying, he picked up the bedclothes from the foot of the bed and hurled them over the deceased's face.

Two seconds later, the 'corpse' sat bolt upright and snatched the bedspread from his face.

'Wassamatter? – Wassgoingon? – Who the bloody hell are you?'

Georgie Pilbeam had returned home earlier that afternoon just after the pubs had shut. Having had a little too much to drink, he had flopped on to the bed, too tired even to close the front door. He was aroused from some very deep slumbers by heavy footsteps. Just as he was about to open his eyes, everything went dark and someone pronounced life extinct.

'Scared the shits outa me I can tell yer,' said George. 'Fort I was in the bleedin' mortuary.'

Dick had unfortunately only climbed to the third floor. His colleagues had gone straight to the correct level and, sure enough, found the grizzly remains of the killer's handiwork. Within a few days 'A man was assisting police with their inquiries.' Needless to say, he was not captured by the crew of 'Mike 3'.

In spite of the drama of both local and national press coverage, TV cameras and radio, the main talking-point at the station that week was Dick pronouncing the drunk 'Well dead!' I have always been highly suspicious of the standard of first-aid practised by most police officers. I have decided that if ever I am involved in an accident and a policeman reckons that I am dead, I will ask for a second opinion. After all, it might be Dick.

Uniform officers, then, are rarely involved in murder

cases. In fact it would not be unfair to say that they have hindered more murder investigations than they have actually assisted, the main reason being that when you are first on the scene, you do not always realize that you are dealing with a murder. It only needs a couple of hippo-footed coppers to clump about over the scene of a crime, no matter how well intentioned, for the arrest to be delayed for ages.

Perhaps the best example of this concerns a policeman at a nearby station who has gone down in crime investigation folk-lore. He was called to a room in which a young girl had been strangled. He was not sure how long she had been dead, so he removed the ligature from her neck in case there was a spark of life. Finding that she was beyond help, he then walked across the room and picked up the telephone to call for assistance, thus violating just about every scene-of-crime rule in the book.

But how do you know if she is beyond help if you don't slacken the cord? Do you just leave her lying there? Perhaps you could explain to her your reasons – 'I'm sorry, luv, I realize that you are dying fast but it's more than my job's worth to loosen the binding from your neck. You might have been bloody murdered.'

Well, there's a nice decision to have to make. If you take the ligature from her neck and she is *just* alive, your picture will be in tomorrow's *Sun* and she will name her next baby after you. But if you take it off and she is *just* dead . . .

9. Horror

The long cold winter had given way to a sunny but windy late March. Wykeham Road railway bridge was bathed in pale spring sunshine as one of the few remaining steam-engines in use on British Railways headed south across its creaking girders. The cinders that fell from its fire-plate lay dormant on the tinder-dry sleeper. The gale-force wind that had swept London for the past three days tormented the ember with a life-and-death struggle. It flickered, faded and flickered again, as it tenaciously clung to life.

I drove the police van across the station yard and on to the washing bay. These vans, sometimes known to older members of the public as 'Black Marias' or 'Hurry-up-vans', were in those days the cornerstone of the force transport. I was early-turn van driver that month (most station duties are done on a monthly basis since this system makes for variety and shares around the work-load). The van driver is a general dogsbody who does any running around which may be necessary. He would rarely deal with emergency calls but would be used for such mundane work as transporting property or animals and picking up drunks from gutters.

Suddenly, Station-Sergeant Rawlings, an elderly, white-haired, pre-war policeman, called out from the front-office window.

'Pop down to number four, Crimea Street. Someone's found an injured alsatian.'

'Thanks,' I replied, 'but I'm not very good with

alsatians, even when they are healthy.'

'Look confident, son! That's all you have to do! Look confident!'

'Can I pick up a PC from a traffic-point? I may need help,' I said appealingly.

'Have a look first, the dog may be dead, then even you can cope. But remember, if it's an animal, don't hang about! If a blind man's wooden legs burst into flames, no one cares. But leave an injured dog for five minutes and people start ringing their MP. Just look confident, son, that's all.'

At 8.30 a.m. I drove out of Wharf Road Police Station into London's morning rush-hour and ten minutes later I turned the van into Crimea Street. The street consisted of two rows of terraced houses that had long since gone to seed. They had been allowed to decay because of the impending redevelopment of the area. Many of our 'problem families' lived in the street and it was very rare that a day would go by without police being called to at least one of them. Each house had a space at the front about two yards square. This had originally been a garden but over the years the gardens had become neglected or vandalized and now they were used for little else except storage. An assortment of barrows, motor bikes, coal boxes or in the case of number four, an old washing mangle, littered the approaches to most houses. Lying against the mangle was the cause of my call, a huge black and grey alsatian. It appeared to take only a minimal interest in me. I walked past and knocked on the filthy green and cream painted door.

It was opened by an enormous middle-aged woman wearing a short-sleeved overall which bit deep into her massive arms. The stale smell from the interior of the house hit me instantly in the face.

'Did you call the police, luv?' I said, pretending I had

not seen the dog.

'Yes, it's 'im,' she replied, pointing to the dog. ''E's been 'ere since late last night. I don't fink 'e's hurt, just tired. He don't belong to anyone round 'ere and 'e ain't got no collar,' she concluded, forestalling just about every question I would be likely to ask.

I bravely stooped to examine the animal which immediately lifted his head, curled back his lips and snarled. White foam ran down from the sides of his mouth and he looked really cross. I could not see any way that I was going to persuade him into my van without help.

'I'll just nip down to Wykeham Road, luv, and pick up a PC from the traffic-point. I'll be back in a few minutes.'

'Don't be bleedin' long, then, I'm waiting to use me mangle.' And with that she slammed the street door.

PC Eddie Benbow looked at his wrist-watch – 8.30 a.m. He groaned to himself. He had been on Wykeham Road point for exactly one hour and still had another ninety minutes remaining. In conjunction with the rest of his colleagues, Eddie hated rush-hour traffic-points. They had many disadvantages. First, they were 'fixed', i.e. one could not be absent without a very good reason. Secondly, one had to take a late breakfast – early-turn started at 5.45 a.m. and there was rarely time to eat before then. And thirdly, one was at the mercy of the elements. Wykeham Road and Old Church Street point had all of these disadvantages, plus the additional one of being a very narrow junction. The slightest deviation from the centre of the road could mean a bus on your foot. So it was with a feeling of some pleasure that Eddie saw a thin swirl of smoke coming from the nearby railway bridge.

The first problem Eddie faced was ascertaining the exact cause of the smoke. He guessed that it was a 'sleeper' fire, which were quite rare nowadays but had been very common a few years previously when the steam engines were in regular use. What he really needed was a vantage point, preferably one that required no climbing. Eddie Benbow was easily the smartest policeman at Wharf Road Police Station. His neatly pressed uniform, clipped military moustache and immaculately polished shoes singled him out from the unmade-bed appearance of many of his workmates. He not only took great pains with his appearance but he also took trouble to preserve that appearance. In Benbow's book climbing was for kids and most certainly not for thirty-three-year-old policemen.

About thirty yards west of the railway bridge stood Stanley House, a four-storey Edwardian tenement. Eddie removed his white traffic gauntlets, folded them carefully, placed them into his jacket pocket and meticulously patted down the bulge until it matched the outline of his uniform. He then climbed the scrubbed stone staircase of Stanley House until he reached the top floor. There was a small north-facing balcony on each level. He immediately realized that the angle was useless for a view of the bridge so he adjusted his tie and knocked, rather officiously, on the door of number forty-seven. It was opened by a tall, rather attractive woman in her early thirties, clad in a pink nylon quilted dressing-gown.

'Could I have a look out of one of your windows, dear? I think one of the sleepers on the bridge is on fire,' said Eddie.

'Certainly,' she replied, 'would you like a cup of tea? I'm just pouring one out.'

Before Eddie answered he looked down at the bridge which was almost beneath him now. He could see that the fire was confined to just one sleeper and did not appear to be in any danger of spreading. In fact, he thought, if left alone it would probably go out of its own accord. He weighed up in his mind what to do: if he left the fire to extinguish itself he would have no excuse for being away from his point. On the other hand, if he called the brigade and made out a report, then there would be time for tea, a fag and a searching conversation with the woman in the pink dressing-gown. Could have possibilities!

'Yes, please, I'd love a cup.'

'Okay, I'll just give the twins their cornflakes, they are at home from school with the 'flu, we've all got it in this house, my old man's in bed with it real bad.'

Eddie gulped; he drank his tea quickly and left. He decided to forget the fire after all. It would soon go out; anyway it had almost stopped smoking.

As I drove down Wykeham Road, I saw Eddie Benbow emerge from the old flats next to the railway. He waved to me and I pulled into the kerb. We both started to talk at once. Eddie, however, was more determined and eventually won by saying:

'As you have appeared on the scene, do you think you could help? There is a slight sleeper fire up on the bridge.'

'Well, I was going to get you to assist me with a maniac dog, but I'll drive to the "nick" first and call the brigade. While they are dealing with the fire, I'll come back and pick you up and we'll tackle this bloody alsatian,' I replied.

I then left Eddie to take up his traffic-point, while I returned to Wharf Road Police Station and telephoned the brigade.

Blue Watch had just begun their tour of duty at nearby Peck Street Fire Station. There had not been time to carry out any of the obligatory daily maintenance when suddenly the teleprinter began to clatter its fateful message. Sleeper fires were fairly straightforward and when I phoned the message through I had emphasized that it was in fact a very small blaze. The usual brigade practice was to send three appliances to all fires, regardless of the nature of the call. The only time I knew them to deviate from this policy was when it was deliberately stressed by police that there was no possibility of a major fire developing. It was obvious, though, that a turn-table ladder would have to be sent, because of the difficulty in gaining access to the elevated line. At the same time that the appliance left the forecourt of Peck Street Fire Station the 8.51 a.m. train from Bromley was four miles away and slowing at the approaches to Nunhead. The southbound 9.01 a.m. was just about to leave Blackfriars, all three destined to meet in a few minutes.

The Wykeham Road bridge was situated on a bend in the line and vision both up and down the track was partially obscured. Fireman Kevin Jones watched as his colleague Peter Masefield held the small hand-pump to extinguish the smouldering sleeper. Kevin's job on this particular fire-duty was to keep a watch for approaching trains. It was strange how one could be just thirty feet above the chaos of one of London's busiest and narrowest roads and yet feel totally removed from the turmoil beneath. If it had not been for the wind, the old bridge would have been quite tranquil in the early spring sunshine.

Kevin felt the vibration and heard the clatter of the approaching Blackfriars-bound train some seconds before he actually saw it. He blew his whistle and the rest of the fire-crew stepped back to allow the train to pass. Men rarely grow out of the fascination of watching trains, and each crew member gazed with no little envy as the blind monster followed the rails north. A fleeting glimpse of a peaked-capped, white-faced driver, raising a hand in apparent acknowledgement, caused most of the crew to wave back. The increase in wind turbulence was literally staggering; the three men standing between the north- and southbound tracks had great difficulty in keeping their feet. It was doubtful if any of that fire-crew even saw the

9.15 a.m. from Blackfriars until it butchered them. Each of the three men ricocheted from the wheels of both trains, backwards and forwards, cutting and gouging, ripping and tearing. The roar of the wind smothered the screams of the men and ten long seconds later, as the trains passed on, the only movement on the bridge was the fluttering of pieces of blood-soaked uniform. Station Officer Hicks, who had survived three years as a Japanese prisoner of war on the Burma–Siam railway, had lasted just three minutes on that south London bridge.

I decided to have a quick cup of tea before I returned to the alsatian. I entered the canteen and found the staff preparing for the inevitable peak period when almost everyone came in at once. The dining area was quiet, however, the only other occupant being Inspector Franks, the early-turn duty-officer, who had just ordered his breakfast. As a supervising officer I found it difficult to communicate with him.

Franks was in his late forties, quite smart in appearance except for his cap which always appeared two sizes too large. He had been an inspector for some years and was obviously destined to remain so for the rest of his service. He was cynical, bitter, sarcastic to an extreme, and I never heard him speak well of anyone. He had, it was rumoured, committed some disciplinary misdemeanour some years past and instead of going on to a higher rank had remained an inspector. I like to think, however, that his inability to obtain a higher rank was simply good judgement by the selection board. Franks considered he was worthy of higher things and also considered that Wharf Road was an area well beneath his social class. If he had one gift, though, it was his ability to depute work. In that he was an absolute master. Some said he could be very competent when he put his mind to it. I knew Franks for six years and never once found out the truth of that thought. He well earned the derisive nickname of 'Worker'.

Suddenly, a young police cadet who had been manning the station switchboard, burst into the room and in an almost hysterical high-pitched voice screamed out:

'Wykeham Road railway bridge, sir! Two firemen have been killed and one badly injured! PC Benbow wants you to attend immediately!'

'Does he now?' said Franks deliberately and softly, 'well, well, and does PC Benbow know that I have ordered my breakfast? Tell PC Benbow from me that if he can't cope, he shouldn't have joined.'

The last part of that remark was classified in the Franks repertoire as humour. It was wasted on me, and the cadet could only stare in amazement.

'Has Benbow got ambulances and fire brigade there?' added Franks.

'Yes, sir!'

'Then he is quite capable of managing. I am going to have my eggs and bacon.' Franks opened his *Daily Mail* to show that as far as he was concerned, the matter was ended.

I said to him: 'Do you want me to go down there?'

'No,' replied 'Worker', 'yours is the only vehicle now available. You'd best stop here.'

Twenty minutes later the extension phone in the canteen rang. It was the coroner's officer. He is a policeman who usually makes arrangements for the removals of bodies from the scenes of fatal accidents.

'Could you please collect the bodies in the police van and take them into the police station while it is decided which mortuary is to receive them? Oh! One more thing – take a shovel!'

Five minutes later I drove out of the station yard and, not surprising, found traffic conditions chaotic. The distance from the station to Wykeham Road was about one mile, yet it must have taken twenty minutes to complete the journey, with traffic rolling forward in fifteen-second bursts. I eventually turned the van into Wykeham Road and I was amazed at the scene in front of me.

The road had been closed to both vehicle and pedestrian traffic. Numerous cars belonging to senior fire chiefs were scattered importantly about. Ambulances and fire-engines were untidily parked and the outer layer of vehicles consisted of three police cars, which almost totally blocked the road. Dominating the whole scene was a huge mobile crane, which had been practically hi-jacked from a nearby construction site. The crane stood in the middle of the road adjacent to the bridge, its jib reaching up beyond the rails. Its heavy hook and cable hung down, swaying slightly in the strong wind as if shaking its head in total disbelief at the sight beneath.

Almost under the bridge stood a solitary unmanned fire-engine. Its radio was blaring metallic messages but there was no one to hear. The cabin door was open and I looked inside. It had the empty desolation of a ghost-ship; somehow one could sense that this was the vehicle which now had no crew.

Already about two hundred people had gathered and they just stood gazing up at the rusty viaduct. The bridge from ground level looked like any of the other fifty bridges on that line. However, nothing is guaranteed to draw the public quicker than the thought of someone else's death. Already the rumours were circulating: *two* firemen cut to pieces is nowhere near as good a story as *twelve* firemen cut to pieces, and so it went on. Each ten minutes that passed saw the mythical demise of yet another man.

After a brief consultation with the senior fire officer present, it was decided that I should reverse my vehicle up to the bridge. The bodies, which had by now been wrapped in a large brown rubber sheet, would be lowered by the crane into the back doors of my van.

Two young policemen had now arrived from their traffic-points, and they began to move the crowds back some sixty yards or so. It was not easy. There had been a slaughter and the crowd wanted to be part of it. They wanted to see it, experience it, talk about it; they wanted to tell their families, their workmates, their customers, their teachers and their pupils. Each of that crowd could smell blood and no boy-of-a-policeman was going to deprive them of their pleasure. I saw one particularly ghoulish woman of about fifty, literally claw her way to the front of the crowd. One of the two policemen yelled to her:

'For God's sake, woman, show some dignity!'

'Wassa matter, mate? What's goin' on?' came the incredible reply.

'Get them all out of the fucking street ! ! !' I looked up at the escarpment and saw Eddie Benbow, ashen-faced and looking ten years older than he had at 6.00 a.m. that morning. The two young policemen holding back the crowd did not really appreciate what had happened up on that bridge; they did, however, recognize the unusual fury in Benbow's voice. This time they were more decisive as they pushed everyone back to the junction of Old Church Street.

I stood on the rear steps of my van and watched as the steel hawser of the crane began to descend to the track above me. Soon the parapet of the bridge hid the hook from my view. The wind seemed momentarily to have abated into a breeze. I listened for sounds from the lines above, but the only noise I could clearly distinguish was the rhythmic grating of a shovel. Noise does not usually bother me but my teeth went instantly on edge.

Eventually, the shovelling stopped and the hawser

began to move. I watched as the cable rewound itself slowly round the spool at the base of the crane. I looked up and saw the huge hook slowly appear from above the bridge. A heavy rope ran down from the hook to a large dark brown package which swung perilously in the early spring sky.

'Ooo look! Those firemen are in that parcel, can you see them?'

I looked to where the voice had come from and I saw a woman in a pink quilted dressing-gown. She stood at an open window in the nearby tenement, and I could just see the heads of two small boys peeping above the sill. By this time the package was just above me. A helmetless fireman appeared on the parapet of the bridge, and in a voice full of emotion he yelled to her: 'What d'ye think this is? A fucking circus? Get those kids in and shut your bloody windows!'

Because of the interruption, my attention had been distracted from the package for some seconds. Suddenly, I was aware that my right wrist was wet. I think I knew the cause before I looked down; the blood, which had begun to seep its way through the folds of rubber, had already covered the shoulder of my uniform and was spattering the rest of my clothing. I frantically signalled to the crane driver and he lowered his grim bundle the few remaining feet. I swiftly pushed it on to the long seat inside the van and slammed shut the door. I ran to the driving seat but for some seconds appeared incapable of finding the correct key to fit the ignition. Eventually I started the engine and slowly threaded my way through the parked vehicles until I reached the main road.

Traffic was now almost solid. I was determined, however, that my return to Wharf Road was going to be much quicker than my trip from it. I drove to the outside of both northbound traffic lanes and put on the van headlights. (This was before the days of the two-toned klaxons.) I weaved in and out of the oncoming traffic, ringing the bell persistently. Three minutes later I drove into the station yard, having left behind me a trail of mass confusion. It was a strange feeling; the cargo of still warm limbs and intestines did not affect me anything like as strongly as the wet blood on my wrist.

I parked the van in the garage in the corner of the station yard. For some unaccountable reason, I locked the doors. I ran to the water-tap in the nearby maintenance bay and thrust my arm under the icy jet. The blood on my hand came off quite easily; the scarlet stain on my shoulder simply diluted and spread. I walked into the front office, just in time to receive a telephone call from Inspector Gunn at the adjacent Peck Street Police Station. He knew me slightly because we both followed the fortunes of Millwall Football Club and had often commiserated with each other on endless black Saturdays.

'I am reporting the incident,' said Gunn, 'will you take the bodies to Low Pond Mortuary?'

'Sure,' I replied, 'but why are you reporting it? It happened well on our manor.'

There was a long pause, then Gunn said softly: 'I went to see if I could give any help, I was the only senior rank present. Franks was conspicuous only by his absence. In my report I will move the location south a little and it will now be reported here, at Peck Street.'

'Franks knew, guv'nor,' I said.

'There is nothing you can tell me about that lazy bastard,' said Gunn coldly, and rang off.

Inspector George Gunn was an extremely competent man but an incident of this nature could easily be a week's work for a duty officer. There would be many unpleasant tasks to perform: post-mortems and inquests to attend, witnesses and relatives to interview, and endless sheets of typescripts to complete. Franks had certainly made yet another enemy, but, nevertheless, he had emerged unscathed again.

The remainder of the early-turn had by now made their way back on foot to the station and were now ordering their breakfasts. All, that is, with the exception of Eddie Benbow who, without speaking to anyone, had gone upstairs to his bunk in the single men's section house. The usual card games were ignored today; the only topic of conversation was the morning's horror. Firemen and policemen have a parallel in much of their work and everyone felt a sense of personal loss. Station-Sergeant Rawlings entered the canteen and said quietly to me: 'The undertakers have arrived. Will you give them a hand?'

I joined the undertaker and his young assistant in the yard and unlocked the doors of the police van. They backed a navy-blue, nondescript truck up as close as possible to my vehicle and removed from it the shell, used for transporting human remains.

Since I had not been up on that bridge at Wykeham Road, I had yet to experience the full horror of that package. The old undertaker cut through the ropes securing the sheet, the pressure of the binding slackened and the bundle moved of its own accord. My stomach lurched as the parcel spread slowly sideways. I had dealt with scores of accidents and numerous deaths already in my police service, yet I just knew that inside that covering was going to be my worst experience to date. I also knew that I was not going to take it very well. That bundle of death was not just in my van, it was entwined in my nerve ends and threatening to explode.

I watched apprehensively as the first layer of the sheet was thrown back. I prepared to retch, but underneath was a second layer; that was thrown back and a round, dark-haired head fell on to my right foot.

'Just a minute, son,' said the old undertaker to the young apprentice, who had been attempting to unravel the gory puzzle, 'if we take out the legs and lift the rubber sheet by its ends, we can slide the remains into the shell.'

We each took a section and endeavoured to tip the contents into the shell. Unfortunately the total weight was too heavy; bits and pieces of men and uniform spewed out all over the floor of the garage. Again the awful sound of that shovel and soon the 'shell' was placed in the truck. The undertaker thanked me for my assistance and he and his lad drove off to Low Pond Mortuary. Just as soon as their truck had left our yard, I began to feel better. A cup of tea! That was what I needed. I walked across the yard towards the canteen; without warning I was violently sick.

About an hour later, the rest of the early-turn shift had returned to the streets and I was hosing out the inside of the police van. The young cadet called out: 'Fire Brigade on the phone for you!' I picked up the telephone in the garage.

'Hullo.'

'Are you the bloke who took our fellows to the mortuary?'

'Yes.'

'Well can we have our sheet and ropes back?'

I could not answer for some seconds. Two of their colleagues killed, one mutilated, and all they are worried about is their bloody sheet and ropes! Is that all the three of them meant? Is that all life is worth? I knew, of course, that I was being unreasonable but for the first time that morning I had something tangible on which to hang my emotions. I tore into the voice on the other end of the line; I was almost grateful to him. I could actually *blame* him. I blamed him for the blood on my hands; the head at my

143

feet; the vomit in the yard. Then I realized I was talking to a dialling tone; he had replaced the receiver. I was instantly ashamed. For all I knew he could have been the best friend of either of the victims. He may have even been up on that bridge. I booked out the van and drove to Low Pond Mortuary.

I entered by the new wing. A modern administration block had been added and it was all strip-lighting, oak-panelling and glass. This new section, however, backed on to the early nineteenth-century original; one stepped back a hundred years by the simple process of opening a door. I walked down a carpeted corridor, past the hand-painted door signs – 'Coroner's Court', 'Pathologists' and 'Coroner's Officers' – to a door marked 'Strictly Private'. On passing through that portal, I entered another corridor; but the whole geography had changed. One first noticed the drop in temperature. The oak-panelling and carpet gave way to glazed tiles and stone slabs. Hanging light-bulbs replaced fluorescent lamps and I felt that I had penetrated a secret Victorian world just a few yards from a busy twentieth-century thoroughfare.

I pushed open the door at the end of the passage and immediately had to leap back to avoid being knocked down. The threat to my person was caused by a steel trolley upon which lay the nude dead body of a woman in her late seventies. She lay on her back with her legs parted. Between her knees lay a dead baby, about three months old. Momentarily I had a grotesque mental picture of a dead woman giving birth to a dead baby. Both corpses had apparently just arrived pending a post mortem. The cheery 'Mornin'' of the attendant acted like a face-slap upon me. The trolley passed by, then I entered the morgue proper.

This room was quite brightly lit, with spotless white tiles throwing back the glare of the fluorescent tubes.

Already the staff were laying out one of the dead firemen. They were piecing him together on the slab like some Frankenstein jigsaw. I asked for the sheet. 'Sorry, but we've been too busy to clean it,' said one of the attendants. I took it soiled.

I decided to call back at Wharf Road Police Station to clean the sheet in the yard. On entering the front office I saw PC Derek Blake, a close friend of mine. It was his birthday and he was wearing a brand new Cambridge-blue cardigan. 'Give me a hand with this sheet, Derek. I cannot return it like this,' I requested. We went into the police stables and carried out the wooden frame upon which the mounted branch clean their horse-harness. I threw the sheet over the frame and Derek picked up the yard broom. I turned on the hose and sprayed the sheet while Derek began to brush it. The small wet stains of blood, bile and urine began reluctantly to fade from the brown rubber. Suddenly a huge gust of wind roared through the yard's double gates; the sheet was lifted, as if by some invisible giant. It appeared to pause for a split second in the air, then it swooped down, wrapping itself completely around Derek! Shuddering violently, he tore frantically at the foul-smelling shawl, and as it finally fell to the ground I could see that his light-blue cardigan was covered with diluted body-stains. He ripped off the garment and threw it instantly in the nearby dustbin. We did not try again to clean the sheet.

We drove the two miles to Peck Street Fire Station in silence. Our journey took us past Wykeham Road bridge. The ambulances and fire-engines had long since left, the crowds had vanished and the trains were running. It was just as if the morning's events had never happened. I did not drive into the fire station yard – I wanted to spend the minimum time there – but just dumped the sheet in the office and almost ran out. I felt that I wanted to keep saying 'Sorry' to everyone. Why are we afraid to show our emotions?

After our return to Wharf Road, I went into the front office to book back my van. I was in time to hear the superintendent saying, 'Why was the accident not reported at this staton, Mr Franks? Surely it was on our manor?' I paused, almost on tip-toe; this should be interesting.

'You are right, sir, it is the incompetence of that cadet on the switchboard. I was never informed until Inspector Gunn had already started to deal with it.'

I stared at Franks in total disbelief, but I knew that I could never shame him. The Frankses of this world believe just what they want to believe and nothing else.

I booked back the van and left the front office. There was a flight of steps leading from the office and down into the yard. The top of these steps was one of the few corners of the old building that could capture the early spring sunshine. I was beginning to wish that I had never given up smoking. I looked across the yard and saw what I first thought to be a rat. We had plenty of these; they came from the stables. I walked stealthily towards it. When I was about ten yards away, I realized that it was simply a grey bloodstained sock, blowing about in the strong wind. I picked it up, intending to throw it in the dustbin. I pulled back my arm to take aim when I became aware that there was something inside the sock. I opened the top but the wool was matted and I could not see down inside. I turned the garment inside-out and two toes fell into my hand.

'Harry!' came the yell from the front office.

'Sergeant!' I replied, almost as loud.

'There's a lady on the phone who reckons no one in her house can have a clean vest until you move that dog.'

Oh Christ! The bloody dog! I had completely forgotten it.

'Well, judging by the smell, the thing must have been in residence for a year, sergeant. I don't suppose another hour's going to make any difference. Tell her I'm on my way.'

10. *Demos*

One recurring theme of present-day policing, particularly in London, is the demonstrations. Almost every weekend throughout the year there are groups of people (often the same ones) marching, meeting, protesting, picketing or simply going along for the walk. A few years ago, I was on duty on four consecutive weekend demonstrations and the banner of the Camden Trades' Council was conspicuous on each of them. As a result of this, I began to feel that it couldn't be a proper demonstration unless the Camden Trades' banner was unfurled.

The average PC tends to become a little blasé about demonstrations, or demos as they are usually known. After a year or so, he has experienced most of them anyway. He probably sees them as little more than an erosion of his weekend and never really understands what they achieve. No matter how worthwhile the cause may be, having to escort a march for two or three miles when the chant is both repetitive and banal does have the effect of blunting one's sympathy. I once marched for two hours alongside some boiler-makers from Birkenhead, whose entire repertoire was 'Heath Out!' which they repeated with equal and unfailing enthusiasm every twenty seconds for two-and-a-half miles. God it was boring!

Most demonstrators are genuinely moved to protest; but some others will join any march, wave any banner and take up any cause. This came home to me in the 'sit-in' at Centre Point in the mid-1970s. I have a great feeling for the homeless; I have in fact been one myself. With the amount of empty property in the capital, I have never been able to understand why anyone should be without a home. Therefore when I heard on the radio one Friday that a group of professional people – lawyers, solicitors, teachers, etc. – had staged an occupation in that mammoth empty tower-block, I was filled with admiration. Centre Point had stood vacant in the heart of London for some years and the value of the building had soared by millions of pounds, simply by being kept empty.

The group astutely announced the time and day that the occupation would end – Sunday at 3 p.m. It worked perfectly. They had maximum coverage from the press, TV and radio, and probably gained more publicity than anyone since John married Yoko. Crowds of people gathered to see them leave the building. People waved from buses, passing cars sounded their horns in support and a festive atmosphere hung over the Tottenham Court Road. My main task that day was simply to ensure the crowd did not spill on to the roadway; but as the group made their exit, my greatest difficulty was to refrain from joining in the rapturous applause.

Suddenly it all went sour. Small-minded rowdies tried to cash in. Their action ruined the whole effect: what had begun as a smooth, professional, well-thought-out action became an absolute shambles. Fights, arguments and scuffles broke out amongst the crowd and a sit-down took place in Tottenham Court Road. Arrests and allegations were made and it was 'rent-a-crowd' at its worst.

Usually demonstrations are fairly well organized, both by the organizing committee and by A8 (the department at Scotland Yard that deals with demonstrations). The two main complaints of the rank and file on these occasions are the sheer monotony and the tendency to over-police.

There is not much that can be done about the first, and the second usually occurs because the march organizers overestimate how many people will attend. This happens time and again. Perhaps if they could be presented with the bill they would be more realistic. In the 1979 pre-election period, the cost of both the National Front and the Socialist Workers' Party must have been astronomic. There were more police used for these two groups than for the three main parties put together. I attended more than a dozen of these extremists' meetings, at places ranging from Southall in the west to Ilford in the east. I did not attend one by the Liberal, Labour or Conservative parties. In the resulting election, the parties that had cost most of the tax-payers' money polled less than two per cent of the total votes!

Ninety-nine per cent of demonstrations are peaceful but just occasionally there will be scuffles; on even fewer occasions, there will be violence. At these rare events, an experienced copper soon learns one very important lesson: avoid the television cameras at all costs! At the Notting Hill carnival in 1978, a contingent of police from Wharf Road was positioned adjacent to a camera site. Over four thousand police were used in policing the carnival, and the total figure for police injuries issued afterwards by Scotland Yard was twenty-one. Thirteen of these were from our station alone, out of a total of fifty men!

Whilst TV cameras usually make a bad situation worse, they pale into insignificance beside any organization with its own camera team. The usual ploy is for these cameras to be focused on a section of the police line. Missiles, or other forms of violence will be offered; the cameras are then switched on to record the reaction of the police. When the film is subsequently shown, the police action comes over not as retaliation but as provocation. It is rather a clever move because even after all these years, if anyone punches me on the nose, my instinctive reaction, I must confess, is to thump him back.

The smooth way in which A8 deals with demonstrations speaks well for its organization. On 28 April 1979 there were several local derby football matches involving London teams, many with both promotion and relegation at stake; a meeting was held at Southall to protest about the death of Blair Peach; and an anti-abortion march of almost twenty-five thousand people, taking nearly three hours to file through, was held in the West End. Just about every single copper who could be used found himself on the streets that Saturday. In spite of all of these commitments, the day passed quietly, all credit being due to the protesters and virtually none, needless to say, to the football fans.

The number of police now needed for football matches is quite ridiculous. Ten years ago I formed the entire police contingent at Dulwich Hamlet football ground for an amateur International match between England and Holland. Nowadays two hundred police are considered a normal number at many of London's football stadiums.

In spite of the smoothness with which crowd operations are usually controlled, there are occasions when they do not go strictly according to plan. All of these times were typified on one mid-May Saturday in 1978. I was required to report to Wharf Road at 9 a.m. and subsequently to Hyde Park for a march to be held by the sympathizers of the Palestine Liberation Organization. My wife and I had tickets to see Helen Reddy at the London Palladium that evening. As I left for work at about 8.30 a.m. she suggested that I should take my ticket with me in case of delay.

'Don't be silly,' I responded. 'The show doesn't start until 9 p.m. Arabs don't like walking that much!'

Nevertheless I agreed to take her advice.

After a short briefing at the station, I was asked to look outside to see if the coach had arrived. It hadn't. At nine-thirty, someone else had a look but still no coach. At ten o'clock a message from Peckham Police Station told us that it had arrived at Peckham by mistake. Well, these things do happen from time to time and no one was very put out. Finally it arrived, and when we had settled on the coach, there was a last count of heads by the inspector in charge before the order was given.

'Okay, driver, Hyde Park, please.'

'Where's dat, sur?' came the surprising reply.

From Wharf Road to the park should take about ten minutes but for some unexplained reason we circled every roundabout twice. On reaching the park, we were due to assemble in the police station for a meal but the driver missed the turn-off and we had to go to the next junction in order to turn around. After a good breakfast our contingent was instructed to join the rest of the coaches that were parked in line, one behind the other, along the North Carriage Road. Once more we overshot. The North Carriage Road is rather narrow and we were obliged to circuit half of the park in order to turn back. It was at this stage that I experienced my first misgivings.

We alighted and sat on the grass under the trees while waiting for the marchers to gather. They held a meeting for about an hour or so and then began to assemble into columns of eight abreast for the planned march. The route prescribed was a fairly short one, straight through the heart of the West End and terminating at the London School of Economics. There all of the marchers would be invited into the school to see a film about Palestine, narrated by Vanessa Redgrave. It seemed that it was going to be a fairly straightforward afternoon.

Elsewhere in the park and just out of our sight, fifty or

so 'Legalize Cannabis' protestors began to have a meeting of their own.

My position in the line-up could not have been worse; I was to march alongside the organizer's loud-speaker van. The sound from these vans is always distorted and one is lucky to finish the day without a blinding headache.

The thousand or so protesters and their escort wound their way slowly along Oxford Street. A barrage of abuse came from the taxis on one side, while on the other side, a tall spindly-built man with a huge ginger beard jogged slowly alongside the procession, every few yards calling out in a loud voice, 'All politics is pig-shit.' I couldn't help but agree.

Two drunks outside a public house in Bloomsbury provided some light relief. They had just one pint of beer and five teeth between them and somehow had the impression that it was a Roman Catholic pageant. Neither could stand very well and they sought support from the pedestrian guard-rails on the pavement outside the saloon bar. The one holding the glass cupped his free hand to his mouth and repeated at the top of his voice, 'No popery! No popery! No popery!' His drinking companion used the opportunity to have a quick swig from the now unprotected glass. The orator suddenly became aware of the theft and, changing his cupped hand into a fist, brought it down smartly on the head of the thief. The Arabs appeared puzzled by the whole proceedings.

There had been the usual hold-ups on the route but by and large it was a well-disciplined parade and we slowly neared the London School of Economics. I thought it would now be safe to anticipate an early finish. On reaching the Aldwych, the marchers dispersed and made their way through the side street into the school, presumably to see their film.

All of the escorting police were now instructed to

return to their transport and stand by. This is usually the prelude to a dismissal. Every other coach was there in line – except ours. One by one, the various units received their dismissal orders and their vehicles drove quickly away from the scene. With just one coach left, our bus came swinging around the corner. 'Sorry, sur, I got lost,' blurted out the driver.

With each serial of men on a demonstration, there is usually one personal radio. This is tuned in to a wavelength that is dealing simply with that particular demonstration and nothing else; therefore it has to be returned to the local station before the coach leaves for home. Just as we were about to leave the Aldwych and return our radio to Cannon Row Police Station, an astonishing call came over the air.

'Urgent assistance required! Two thousand protesters marching on Buckingham Palace!'

Who the hell were they? Our Arabs had all dispersed and, in any case, that wasn't their scene.

'Right, Paddy,' said Inspector Edwards, 'Buckingham Palace as quickly as possible!'

'Where's dat, sur?' came back the predictable reply.

From the Aldwych to Buckingham Palace is about a mile and the journey is almost a straight line. However this was mid-May and The Strand was full of traffic and pedestrians, most of them foreign. The traffic-lights at the junction of Waterloo Bridge and The Strand changed to red just as we reached the stop-line. 'You're okay, Paddy,' chorused out someone from the back of the coach, 'you're a police vehicle now – Eeee-oar! Eeee-oar! Eeee-oar!' The cry was taken up by the remainder of the coach and the vehicle sped on through The Strand traffic. We collected a couple of lanterns from the road-works outside Charing Cross Station but otherwise we managed to reach Trafalgar Square quite intact.

'Where now, sur?' said Paddy, who had obviously got the feeling for the whole thing.

'Dead ahead! Through those gates!' said Edwards.

Admiralty Arch leads from Trafalgar Square into the Mall and it contains three huge iron gates. The left one leads into the Mall, the right one leads out of the Mall, and the centre one is permanently closed.

'Which gate, sur?'

'The middle one!' yelled the joker from the back.

'Christ, don't tell him that, he'll take it!' said an alarmed voice from somewhere at the front of the coach.

'Left, man, left,' snapped Inspector Edwards.

We roared down the Mall with Paddy clinging determinedly to the wheel.

We swung round the Victoria Memorial and there in front of the palace gates were swarms of the scruffiest people that I have ever seen in my life. The 'Legalize Cannabis' protesters were having a quick 'demo' of their own!

They were not seeking a confrontation, however, and they soon made off towards Trafalgar Square, travelling along the route in fact that we had just taken. They apparently intended to stage a 'sit-down' of some sort on Horse Guards Parade. Once more we all piled into the coach. Leap-frogging the marchers, we formed a cordon across the road that leads from the Mall to Horse Guards Parade. The marchers by this time had no sense of order and they were spread all over the place. They straggled out for about a quarter of a mile, both on the pavement and in the road, but again they avoided us. This time they moved on to Downing Street. Again we piled back into the coach.

'Downing Street, quickly, Paddy,' said Edwards.

'Where's dat, sur?' chorused half the coach.

'Head them off at the pass, sheriff,' came a helpful anonymous yell from the back.

Some three minutes later, we formed a cordon across the entrance to Downing Street.

'We've got to break this lot up into groups, otherwise we'll be sodding about here all night,' said Inspector Edwards.

All night! I thought. What about my Helen Reddy ticket?

The protesters were beginning to lose both their way and their enthusiasm. Many began to drift down the side streets and would soon be asleep on the benches and gardens alongside the river.

Seeing that Downing Street was well covered, a hard-core of about one hundred moved on to the Houses of Parliament. A Morris Dance team was giving a display on the parliament forecourt in front of several hundred spectators, mainly Japanese tourists. The cannabis marchers decided they would go no further. With people now spilling out from the pavement and blocking the roadway, the traffic in Parliament Square became jammed solid. The Morris Dancers, believing that they had their biggest audience for years, threw themselves into their movements with a renewed frenzy. I was suddenly aware of the sound of singing and, emerging from Great College Street, came a Christian Aid procession of about 150 good souls.

I have never seen such confusion. The bells on the legs of the Morris Dancers began to ring more slowly as the crowd thickened. The click of camera shutters and the sound of Japanese voices almost drowned the hymn that was rising from the procession. Helen Reddy seemed a million light-years away.

My personal feelings were that it would have been a good move to leave the confusion to find its own salvation. After all, the cannabis marchers, never the most athletic of protesters, were on their last legs. The Morris

Dancers didn't look too good either. The delight on the faces of the tourists was matched only by the dismay of the Christian Aiders. I was pretty sure that if we ignored it all, it would certainly go away.

It was now well after five o'clock and we also had had a long day. In addition, needless to say, our coach had disappeared again. We had left it parked opposite Downing Street and now it was no longer there. We had overlooked the fact that between Downing Street and the Houses of Parliament, all of four hundred yards, lay Parliament Square. The Square is a rather large round-about and, having taken the wrong road off it, Paddy was apparently trying to make his way back from Victoria. The mass of people outside Parliament had now stopped all the traffic in Westminster and Paddy was marooned half a mile away, somewhere outside Scotland Yard.

Slowly the crowd thinned until it was obvious that few more than fifty or so cannabis marchers were left. Our coach crept slowly around Parliament Square and we wearily climbed aboard, leaving just a few constables behind to supervise the disappearing throng.

'As long as they keep moving they're okay,' said Edwards. 'Six of you escort them, the rest of us will follow at a distance.'

I began to feel a little happier. The marchers crossed St James's Park and slowly climbed the Duke of York steps, with six tired constables trailing behind. Even Paddy's coach couldn't negotiate the steps and we detoured through Trafalgar Square and into Pall Mall, intending to join the group at the top of the wide stone staircase.

The banter in the coach had now ceased. Several men were asleep and the thought in everyone's mind was how soon would we be away? We had expected to see the remnants of the marchers straggling along Pall Mall but all we could see were several bystanders gazing intently down towards the Duke of York steps. As we approached, the top of the staircase took on the appearance of the saloon-bar in Dodge City; all hell was loose. Everyone seemed to be fighting everyone else and somewhere in the middle were six coppers.

As we arrived the crowd scattered in all directions, leaving behind just the wounded for capture. My first reaction was surprise because cannabis marchers are not usually violent. They may bore you to death, with their incessant and obligatory guitars, but they are usually peaceful people.

Two of the policemen had bloody noses but no serious injuries. The same could not be said for the remainder. Several had obviously received a rather heavy thumping. The reason had nothing to do with the police at all. A gang of about a dozen teenagers had happened to be walking down the Duke of York steps as the protesters were going up. The cannabis users looked something out of the ordinary, which somehow seemed a good enough reason for the youths to assault them, so they did. Like sparrows attacking a canary and and with about as much logic.

I groaned in self-pity. We now had four prisoners. They would have to be taken to Cannon Row and charged. We would then have to wait for the arresting officers to finish their paperwork before finally leaving for our own station.

When we eventually arrived back at Wharf Road, I was the first off the coach. A quick wash and change and thirty minutes later I was back in the West End.

I was not the only late arrival that evening, at the upper-circle door at the Palladium. There were a dozen or more people queueing while the attendant searched the ladies' bags and coats. Suddenly there was a crash of breaking glass and I turned to see four drunken supporters of St Helens who had lost at Wembley that afternoon in the

Rugby League Cup Final. They were picking up milk bottles and just tossing them gaily into the air.

'Typical!' said a middle-aged. back-combed, over-weight blonde in front of me. 'Blind-bloody-drunk in the West End of London and not a policeman in sight! I often wonder where they all get to, you can never find one when you need one!'

'They're too bloody tired to get out of their panda cars, I suppose,' I answered treacherously.

Oh Miss Reddy! I love you but if only you knew the trouble I had to see you.

11. *Some Dogs . . .*

The large white flakes had been slanting and swirling across the metropolis for the whole of that Sunday; few people had ventured out. Cars would not start, cinemas were as empty as churches, and aunties remained unvisited. The reluctance of people to leave their homes had given the suburbs a desolate and wintry charm. The footprints left by the early-morning milkmen were soon covered by fresh snow. Fluffy white branches spread out from the trunks of the laburnum trees and romantic souls gazed wistfully through the windows of their centrally heated, double-glazed homes.

The Wharf Road neighbourhood was, however, its customary mess. Saturday's drizzle still lay in pools when Sunday's snows had begun. The rain puddles quickly evolved into a swamp of thick grey icy slush. In addition to the weather, the local dustmen were in the throes of one of their regular strikes. Sinister-looking black plastic bags stood clustered together in dumb conversation on street corners and around lamp-posts.

David Taylor and his police dog 'Hutch' had been on duty at Wharf Road Police Station since early that morning and Hutch was showing some signs of agitation. He was a young dog, potentially excellent but as yet inclined to be inconsistent. He would perform marvellous feats and then, just like a child, he would act as if he had had enough of being good for one day and completely shatter David's complacency. It was approaching the end of Hutch's working day and the dog knew it. He always had his one daily meal immediately after he arrived home, and it was fairly obvious where his canine thoughts lay at that moment.

It had been a very quiet day for crime, the criminals as usual going to ground immediately the cold weather struck. Together with another dog and handler from Peckham Police Station, David had begun the day by patrolling in the 'dog-van'. This vehicle covered the whole of the surrounding district and at times would respond to calls from all over the south-east of London. The two handlers would sit in the front of the van taking turns to drive, and the dogs would be caged in the back.

By about 1 p.m. the road conditions had become so bad that both men decided to split forces. They returned to their own stations and operated directly from there. Hutch, being little more than a puppy, hated this inactivity. At the slightest excuse, he would leap up from the prone position that David had sentenced him to in the corner of the canteen and greet each newcomer with a plaintive, hungry look. On finding that there were no tit-bits being offered, he would slink reluctantly back to his corner and bury his head sadly between his front paws. He was an actor, that dog.

'Right, Hutch! Home for din',' said David eventually.

Whilst these words hardly constituted any Metro-politan Police official dog command, they were always more eagerly obeyed than any 'Heel', 'Hold' or 'Stay'. Within seconds, Hutch had bounded out of the building and into the yard. There he sat impatiently at the rear door of David's old estate car.

'David!' called out the young recruit who was assisting in the front office, 'station officer sez can you 'ave a quick look for this missing kid before you go home? He's only four years old and he's believed to be somewhere local. He knows you are off duty but the weather is too bad to try to get a dog from anywhere else,' he added, forestalling David's obvious first line of defence.

David groaned. A 'missing child' search could take anything between ten minutes and several days and, on some occasions, even weeks. In dog-handling parlance there was no such thing as 'a quick look'.

'Okay,' sighed David, 'give me the details.'

'He's a four-year-old West Indian kid, he's been away since yesterday evening but they only reported him missing half an hour ago.'

'Has someone taken him?' asked David.

'No, he misbehaved so his mother walloped him. He just took off and he hasn't been seen since. That's about all there is to it,' said the recruit.

Both dog and handler squeezed into the rear of a panda car and soon reached the location. It was a housing estate that comprised six blocks of twenty-storey flats. Winston, the missing boy, lived on the tenth floor of one of these blocks.

As the panda braked to a halt in the forecourt of the flats, so Hutch seemed to get the devil in him. First he would not get out of the car, and David had to coax, threaten and finally drag him from the vehicle. Then he ran off up the staircase of the nearest flats, which really made David furious. Because of the weather and the fact that it was now dark, there were few members of the public about to see his embarrassment, but it was nevertheless a blow to his professional pride.

He called to Hutch repeatedly but to no avail. He was not even sure exactly where the dog had gone. Following into the block, he was able to see the wet footprints leading up the rarely used staircase. At each landing, David paused to call Hutch's name but his voice just became hoarser. Suddenly, between the fifth and sixth floors, he saw Hutch standing indecisively; the dog turned first one way and then the other. Swearing profusely, David reached out to place the stout choke-chain around the dog's throat. It was at this moment that Hutch arrived at whatever decision it was that was bothering him and he raced away up the staircase again.

'Christ! I'll kill that bloody animal when I catch him,' yelled David.

'*If* you catch him!' gasped Bill Radcliffe, the panda driver, who was struggling along two flights below.

The dog's paws had now dried and no longer provided any useful tracks. By the time he had reached the twelfth floor, David had slowed to a walking pace; he was therefore able to hear Bill Radcliffe's weak voice from two floors below.

'Dave, I think there is something here!'

He ran back down the stairs and found Bill pointing along the landing. There, alongside the communal rubbish chutes, was an assorted pile of bags and boxes. Sitting quietly beside the pile and gazing at the pair of them in a most disinterested fashion was Hutch. There was no other exit from the landing and David positioned himself in the middle of the walkway, just in case the dog attempted to rush past him. The animal made no such move.

Slipping the lead on to the dog's collar, David moved away towards the staircase, snapping out the command – 'Heel!' Hutch would not be moved. David tugged repeatedly on the chain and the animal hunched his back and attempted to dig in his paws as he began to slip on the smooth concrete floor of the landing.

'What's that, Dave?' said Bill Radcliffe, pointing between two black plastic bags.

A small dark figure lay huddled in the rubbish. Winston Earl Clement Stanley St Luce Robinson was fast asleep amongst the refuse and seemingly none the worse for his experience. David looked down at Hutch: 'How the hell did you know that?' He asked the question so intently that it seemed that he was expecting an answer. Hutch slowly stood up, shook himself, and looked up at David as if to say, '*Now* can we go home?'

There was no reason at all why the dog should have found the boy so quickly. He'd had no clothing to sniff, he had never seen the child before, but nevertheless, within thirty minutes of being reported missing, Winston Earl, etc., etc., was reunited with his mother. It did not always happen this way.

I suppose at this stage I should admit that I am not an animal lover. I could never have been a dog-handler if my life depended on it. I feel that most animals really hate us and, given the chance, police dogs (and horses) carry this feeling to extremes.

Given half a chance, and if one is silly enough to let them, most dog-handlers will bore the pants off you, talking about the magnificent obedience shown by their charges. Each is convinced that his dog is a combination of Rin-Tin-Tin, Lassie and possibly Batman. These dogs, according to their handlers, will separate the good from the bad; stand angelic guard over lost babes; tear murderers limb from limb; scale walls; read and tell the time. I, on the other hand, have been chased by them whilst searching premises; been bitten by them whilst struggling with burglars; and stunk out by them in various police cars. They have eaten my sandwiches, vomited on my tunic and urinated down my legs. I sometimes feel that police dogs are the reincarnation of master-criminals, seeking revenge for their original incarceration or premature death. My first introduction to them is so clearly engraved on my mind.

An early-morning office-cleaner had called into the station to say that she had just seen a man scale the wall of a nearby factory. Together with Inspector Baker five of us went to the scene and began to search the premises. Baker was a very popular man who looked like everyone's idea of an old-time copper. He was a little over six feet in height, with a large belly, full moustache and a deep, gruff voice. We soon found the suspect, who was about to remove the safe. It was thought extremely unlikely that he attempt such a project on his own, so the search was renewed for an accomplice. In spite of the fact that we searched every part of the premises two or three times, no trace of any other villain could be found.

'He's never gonna do that job on his own,' said Baker, 'there has simply got to be another bloke hiding out somewhere in that building.'

'How about calling for a police dog to search for him?' suggested George Rearsden. 'They keep one in Hyde Park at night, it wouldn't take him too long to get here,' he added.

I was sent back to Wharf Road on my cycle in order to contact Hyde Park police and obtain the services of the dog. It appeared that few policemen had heard of this animal or his handler, because he had been waiting for over a week and this was the first time he had been called out.

'If you think that you really need us, we'll be there in about fifteen minutes, always providing that we can get a lift,' said the handler.

I had assumed that because of his inactivity he would be bursting for some excitement. I was therefore surprised at the lack of enthusiasm in his voice. I was soon to find out why.

I pedalled quickly back to the warehouse and gave Inspector Baker the news.

'So we are going to get a dog, eh?' he said thoughtfully. After a second or two, he looked at me and added, 'I suggest you watch carefully, lad, you'll probably learn something – might stand you in good stead in your future police career.'

'Yes, sir,' I dutifully answered.

Some fifteen minutes later, a huge old Wolseley saloon car screeched to a halt outside the warehouse gates. An enormous dog placed its head out of the open rear window and barked at everything in sight. The front passenger door of the car opened and the handler emerged – somewhat tiredly, I felt. He searched his pockets dramatically, as if seeking some vital equipment. Deep inside his jacket he appeared to find the object of his hunt. Carefully slipping his hands from his clothing, he slowly and deliberately rolled himself a cigarette!

'What's your dog like, mate?' asked Inspector Baker.

'He's red 'ot with cats, guv'nor,' came the astonishing reply.

The stage was set, the audience was waiting. We were not to be disappointed. The handler took an extra long draw on his fag, closed his eyes in silent prayer, opened the car door, and the dog immediately fell out on to the pavement.

Exactly on cue, a large ginger tom-cat, which, being an interested spectator, decided that it was time for a little audience participation. It leapt from the pillar of the warehouse gates and slowly sauntered down the road towards Kennington, its tail held rigidly in the air. The dog, which had by this time rolled off the pavement and into the kerbside, now found himself upside down under the car. In his struggles to get free, he obviously rubbed against the very hot exhaust pipe. It must have been at about this moment that he saw the cat for the first time; he instantly went berserk. With a barrage of barks, yelps and screeches, he emerged from under the vehicle with about two pints of Castrol running down his back and hammered down Kennington Road in pursuit of the cat. Pussy turned casually left into an alley and the dog, having overshot the entrance by a full ten yards, skidded to a halt, turned and resumed the chase.

The handler slowly shook his head, relit his drooping cigarette and walked, rather tiredly, in the direction taken by the animals, saying, almost to himself, 'Why does he *always* do that?'

My first introduction to the use of dogs for police purposes was not very impressive, you may think. Well, it was, of course, very early days. Since then I have seen the dog-handling section of the police flourish to become the professional department that it is today. However, policemen of my length of service, having seen the whole evolution of the section, have had many occasions to wonder just whose side the dog was on. Much of the value of dogs in police work has been purely their psychological effect. For instance, a colleague of mine arrived at a tailor's shop at two in the morning to find three men just finishing their pre-Christmas shopping. Each man ran off in a separate direction with an armful of suits. The dog barked furiously and the handler called, 'Stop! Or I'll let the dog go!!' The men stopped instantly. Three shop-breakers were therefore arrested by a dog that never left the handler's side.

On another occasion, I was walking with a friend of mine, Ben Norman, and his dog Max. We suddenly ran into a crowd of about forty to fifty teenagers, all armed to the teeth with coshes and chains. They were apparently one side of an intended multiple gang-fight. As we approached them, they showed no signs of giving ground. Ben was able to excite Max into a fury with a few simple commands and before we had covered forty yards, I was extremely pleased to see the first of the lads begin to run. Within seconds they had all scattered, leaving the street littered with an assortment of weapons.

In those days Max was quite a unique dog. He would respond to an increase in the engine revs of the police car. As soon as the car increased speed, Max would sit bolt-upright on the back seat and emit the most terrifying growls and barks. If one assumes that he was not simply passing an opinion on the standard of driving, then it was a fair bet that he associated the extra speed with a subsequent emergency call.

This was not without its disadvantages. Late one evening, while chasing a stolen car at high speed along Clapham Road, a huge petrol-tanker turned across our path and stalled. I braked as hard as possible but, even though the road was dry, the Wolseley locked into a skid. It was the only time in my life that I was convinced I was going to die. It was pretty obvious that Max was of the same opinion. We finally screamed to a tyre-melting halt six inches from the side of the tanker. Max by this time had somersaulted over the front seats and was now lying on his side biting everything within reach, namely my legs. I must admit that this did not seem to upset him on future calls, although I made sure that from then on he sat behind the radio operator.

As the advantages of dogs became more and more appreciated, tough reliable animals such as Max were in demand for a variety of occasions. They were used to search for explosives long before other dogs were specially trained for this task. Sometimes the Flying Squad (or Sweeney as they are usually known) would use both dog and handler for a specific job. They would perform the required task and return to their own station the following morning, bearing out the old story, I suppose, that every dog has its day. Max in fact had many days. One of the more remarkable culminated in an unusual chase. Handlers are reluctant to let their dogs from their leads but sometimes they have no choice. One of the Flying Squad assignments found the suspect running down an alley at the rear of some terraced houses, hotly pursued by Max. Realizing that the dog was gaining fast, the villain ran into a back garden and then through the back door of the house. The family were just sitting down for tea when suddenly the door burst open. A sturdy, wild-eyed, breathless stranger ran straight through the kitchen-diner and out through the front of the house. Before they could make a move, there was a great barking and Max also ran through in hot pursuit. Seconds later, Ben chased through after Max and at about ten-second intervals, a procession of members of the Sweeney also raced through the house. No one stopped to explain, no explanation was sought!

Max was not the only Wharf Road dog to have his day. David Taylor's first summer as a handler coincided with a temporary shortage of personnel in the Dog Section. He was told that the following two nights he would be on duty in the grounds of Buckingham Palace. Being a fairly young handler, he considered that he had finally arrived. After all, he was very much the new boy, yet here he was, with his dog Hutch, and expected to look after the welfare of the Royal Family. During the hours of darkness, he wandered the grounds of the palace and pried into every intriguing corner. As the early sun began to climb over the Royal Mews, David and Hutch walked the banks of the lake. It was a calm, windless morning and David, a keen fisherman, was eager to see just what kind of fish swam in the royal waters. Suddenly his thoughts were shattered by a hell of a commotion. Blood and feathers were everywhere. The sound of barking and squawking echoed across the lake and around the palace – Hutch had killed a duck! Panic-stricken, David looked quickly up at the windows. He'd half expected the Queen to be standing there shouting 'Off with his head!' He spent the next twenty minutes picking up feathers and putting them in his pockets. The duck he buried quickly and unceremoniously. The following night, when he reported for his second royal duty, he was quite relieved to hear that there was not to be a search party for the royal duck. Hutch had done it again!

12.　. . . and a Few Horses

A street copper works a great deal in conjunction with police dogs. He works hardly at all with police horses. The Mounted Branch are totally removed from ordinary beat duty. One sees them at football matches, demonstrations and many other crowd-drawing functions but one never really works closely with them. They are an entirely separate unit and although I have spent my entire police service on the streets of London, I have worked with them on just one occasion. That was the evening after an England v. Wales rugby match at Twickenham.

The match is a biannual affair and numerous Welsh supporters save their money for two years simply to get fleeced in the big city. Just about everybody has them over, from the ice-cream sellers to the massage-saunas. In an effort to gain their revenge they occasionally make an attempt to capture the Eros statue in Piccadilly Circus. Police are there to see that they do not succeed.

At these times the crowds on the footway become so tightly packed that they have to be eased away, more for their own safety than anything else. If we as foot coppers fail to do this, a couple of horses and riders will easily accomplish it, by gently walking sideways on the pavement at right-angles to the kerb. This is a fairly straightforward operation and is usually managed without any great difficulty. On this occasion, however, loud protests were made by a little square-shaped man who had been complaining about everything and everyone for the previous two hours. Every time he stepped into the road, he was first asked, then subsequently led, back on to the pavement. 'I'm reporting you to the Chief Constable of Carmarthen!' he kept repeating. So saying, he would write down the number of the offending officer on his rugby programme.

The movement of any crowd causes a certain amount of positional change. One moment someone is immediately in front of you, a few minutes later they are several feet away. This was the case with 'Taff the Moan'. He began the evening at least three yards away from me; eventually he was anchored firmly in front of me. He looked at my number and checked his list. I wasn't on it.

'I'm reporting you as well – you're a party to all this!' he bellowed.

He bent his head forward to write down my number, when suddenly an arm came over my left shoulder, a hand snatched the programme smoothly away from the writer and disappeared instantly behind me. The whole operation was accomplished so quickly that 'Taff' did not even know which direction his programme had travelled.

'Who's got it? Come on, who's got it?' he demanded, looking all about him.

The crowd and the police were equally fed up with him and he received no help from either quarter. I was aware of another rapid movement again from behind me, and I saw the remnants of his programme fluttering down around him.

'It's my programme!' he screamed. 'Torn to bloody shreds, man!'

With that he burst into tears!

'I have to present that programme to my wife when I get home, otherwise she will never believe that I have been to the rugby!' he whined.

He desperately sought a replacement from the throng of

people about him but to no avail.

I turned around in an effort to see who the culprit may have been and was taken aback to see no one there except for a police horse and rider. The rider had a bland, expressionless face that conveyed nothing to me. The horse, however, had such an air of superiority that I almost had doubts. No, it couldn't possibly be? After all, I had definitely seen a hand snatch that programme, and only a hand could have torn it up. I looked again at those eyes. They were brown pools of pure innocence, no living creature could be *that* innocent.

An hour or so later, the crowd had almost disappeared in order to catch the twelve-twenty-something from Paddington. Policemen gathered and chatted in small groups. Standing on the corner of Regent Street, I saw two horses and their riders engaged in quiet conversation. I approached one of the riders.

'How did you manage to reach that bloke's programme from where you were sitting?' I asked curiously.

'Not me, mate,' he answered cheerily; then leaning down towards me he added in a quiet confidential tone, 'But I tell you what, you haven't half got to watch 'im.'

He patted the animal's neck in a knowing manner. He then gave me a slow wink and turned and resumed the conversation with his colleague.

It is this pure innocence of horses that makes me so suspicious of them. They look at you with those great soulful eyes and you can never begin to imagine the villainy that goes on behind them. When a horse causes or commits a calamity, it does so in such a manner that the rider seems the only person to blame. Personally, although I am not at all keen on horses, I have nothing but admiration for their shrewdness. Many years ago there was a song entitled 'Horses Don't Bet on People. Horses

Have Too Much Sense'. That sums up the breed perfectly. We always assume that the rider is the intelligent member of the duo. Yet it is a fact that no horse has lost as much as a carrot through betting on people.

I saw an example of this shrewdness during a visit by the president of Portugal. It is one of the peculiar require-ments of the police force on ceremonial occasions that senior officers of the rank of commander and above are usually mounted on horseback. Some of these gentlemen are complete equestrians, taking on a whole new image when mounted upon their chestnut mare. They cut dashing figures reminiscent of Errol Flynn in *Charge of the Light Brigade*. Others, of course, look like sacks of ferrets.

When the royal procession set off on the trip from the palace to Victoria Station, it was obvious that the last time our commander was mounted on any animal at all was probably the little grey donkey that plies between the pier and the lifeboat station. He just did not have a clue how to 'steer' the beast. On the outward journey from the palace he sat as stiff as a board, tugging first one way then the other. The horse did not show any emotion at all; it simply bided its time until the procession was returning. When the column reached the Victoria Memorial in front of the palace, it forked left. That is, with the exception of the commander. His mount forked right. Nothing he could do with the reins made any difference whatsoever.

It was obvious from the animal's demeanour that this was no spur-of-the-moment job. It was a superbly timed and brilliantly executed retribution. The ranks of the crowd parted as the horse advanced towards them, then closed again after the pair had gone through. This placed the constables lining the route in something of a dilemma; should we run after the commander and assist him by about-turning his horse? Or should we face the crowd and not look to the front, as we had been ordered? We decided, rightly I believe, to face the crowd; but as a result, we could not hear the frantic calls for help, nor see the vain struggle with the bridle. I must confess that at this late stage, I did momentarily peep out of the corner of my eye to see the pair advancing up Constitution Hill in the direction of Hyde Park. Unlike the 'Grand Old Duke of York', of course, our hero was entirely on his own. This was somewhat embarrassing for the commander because the main body of the procession was at that moment entering the forecourt of the palace.

In the everyday hurly burly of street duty, one obviously deals with some incidents that are almost repetitive. A policeman may not be called to a fire, for example, for two or three years, then he may find he deals with three in a week. The same applies to accidents. However long the gap between these incidents – weeks or years – the work done at the scene and perhaps afterwards, remains in the memory. One does, though, tend to become more proficient at some things than at others.

If you have been called to a couple of sudden deaths in the space of a few days, when the inevitable third one arrives, not necessarily on your beat, people tend to say: 'Oh give it to him, he's pretty good with sudden deaths.' Of course you are not really 'pretty good with sudden deaths' – it is just that you have had the experience of dealing with them. This, I suppose, is what street duty is all about – experience. What happens, though, when something takes place of which neither you nor any of your colleagues have any experience at all? An accident involving an animal, say? Perhaps even a police animal? It can be quite perplexing; and if there is no one whose knowledge is greater than yours, it can be positively alarming.

Inspector Blackwell knew that horses were pretty

handy for roses and rhubarb but other than that his equestrian knowledge was about nil. There was no good reason why it should have been otherwise. With the exception of the occasional junk-man, one never sees a horse commercially in London. It is true that years ago at police training school each recruit was issued with form 29, required if a horse had to be destroyed in the street. But that practice had disappeared with the horse; or so he thought.

Like most of his colleagues, Blackwell had found the Mounted Branch to be one of the mysteries of life. The very nature of their job seemed to make them aloof. Foot constables are down there in the gutter; horse riders are up there, much nearer heaven. They sit astride their steeds, caps and eyes to the fore, their bottoms beating a quick rhythm, counterpointed by the clip-clop of the animals' hooves. They appear to be a smooth, professional organization. Every eventuality is doubtless catered for in their suave set-up.

One such smoothie was cantering along a back street, not too far from Wharf Road, when suddenly his mount's front right leg was struck and broken by a passing vehicle. The horse stood quietly on three legs by the side of the road and the local copper, who was originally called upon to deal with the incident, decided rather shrewdly that an accident with a police horse should best be dealt with by someone of higher rank than himself. So around the middle of the afternoon, Inspector John Blackwell emerged from a police car and obtained his first view of Dobbin.

It did not require a veterinary surgeon to see that the leg was indeed broken; it hung sickeningly down, clearing the ground by about one inch. The basic rules of first-aid could not very well be used on a horse. To play for time until the ambulance arrived by pouring great cups of hot sweet tea down the patient's throat was really not on. Inspector Blackwell returned to the car and contacted information room at Scotland Yard. He stressed the urgency of the situation and requested the attendance of a vet as soon as possible. By the use of his personal radio, he also contacted Wharf Road and explained that he fully expected to be engaged at the scene for some time, should he be needed.

A few minutes before the accident had taken place, a police horse-box on its way to Epsom had, by some cruel twist of fate, passed by the very spot. Unfortunately the radio in the vehicle was not switched on, so there was no response to an 'all-cars' call over the air for assistance. This was not altogether surprising – one can go for years and never hear a call for a horse-box – they are hardly in constant demand. Sadly, as the minutes ticked by, the box became further and further away from the very spot it was needed most.

Nearly an hour elapsed, with little more to show than an endless procession of people bearing gifts – tufts of grass (from God knows where) and saucers of oats straight from their cereal packets. John Blackwell again called information room. He was reassured to hear from them that Wharf Road police were making all the necessary arrangements. As an afterthought, he called Wharf Road to find out exactly how far the 'necessary arrangements' had progressed. 'Don't worry,' he was told, 'information room have the matter well in hand!' Two great minds without a single thought.

Some twenty minutes later, as if to prove that all was not lost, a car drew up and out stepped a man with a black bag who introduced himself as a veterinary surgeon. He had been called, he said, in the absence of his official police counterpart. After a short examination of the animal, he stated that it could be saved but would require a long period of medical care. The pressing need at that moment was for a horse-box to take the poor creature to the police riding school at Imber Court, some fifteen miles away. The vet then presented a chitty for a hefty bill and left the scene.

The silent horse-box had by this time reached its destination at Epsom, a full hour's drive away. When the news that he was required to return across south London, this time in the rush-hour, was bravely broken to the driver, he was not amused. This reluctance seemed to manifest itself when the engine blew up on the Sutton by-pass.

Now the driver of any of the public services, be it police, fire, ambulance, or even the armed forces, will tell you how difficult it always seems to be to obtain a replacement vehicle. No matter how common the model, it is a statutory practice of all vehicle depots to be out of stock of the particular means of transport that you so desperately need. If this is the case with small, mundane saloon motor cars, it obviously reaches nightmare proportions if one requires a horse-box. A Polaris missile could be procured with less effort. Optimistic moves were nevertheless made to secure such a prize (a horse-box, not a missile) and after patient, diligent inquiries, a horse-box and driver were eventually found – at Epsom. The daylight that was gradually appearing at the end of the tunnel was unfortunately fading fast at the scene of the accident. Murmurings could be heard from horse-loving members of the public.

A further car arrived and out stepped another gentleman with a black bag. He was, so he said, the official police vet. He gave the horse a quick examination, then promptly shot it! This placed Inspector Blackwell in rather an interesting predicament; he now had a horse-box on the way to collect a dead horse. Such vehicles are functional; they are ideal for a horse that is fine, healthy and upright but more than useless when the horse is dead, heavy and horizontal. Fearing another engine explosion (the second horse-box was, after all, using the same by-pass), an urgent call was sent requesting that the box return to its base.

The next move was to obtain the services of a knacker. Within a short space of time, news reached John Blackwell that the horse-box was now safely back in base. Unfortunately the knacker had left his, to spend some time in Ipswich, and he was not expected back until the following morning. Contrary to popular belief, knackers are not common in London nowadays. The inspector now pondered over his fresh problem, how to dispose of a very dead horse in a very dark Peckham?

In a sudden flash of inspiration, someone suggested a low-loader. Of course! If they can remove immobile vehicles, why not dead horses? A quick telephone call to the district garage soon told him why not.

'Not our job, mate, we remove motors – not mokes,' said the civilian employee.

Up until this moment, in spite of all of the frustrations that had arisen, Blackwell had been the very epitomy of what professional middle-management should all be about; his calm, imperturbable approach had been remarkable. It had, however, not achieved very much. Perhaps now the time was ripe for some carefully planned hysteria. He called Wharf Road on his personal radio.

'I want a driver to go to the district garage and confiscate the first low-loader he sees. If anyone tries to stop him – nick him!'

'Nick him?' echoed the Wharf Road operator. 'What for?'

'Causing unnecessary suffering to a dead horse!' came back the astonishing answer.

'But how can you cause a dead horse unnecessary – ?' The reply cut off in mid-sentence. Inspector Blackwell had now been standing in that street for three-and-a-half hours; if he had reached the stage where he was demanding the nicking of someone for 'causing unnecessary suffering to a dead horse' then young 'Butch' Devonshire on the switchboard at Wharf Road was not going to be the one to argue with him.

With the arrival of the police driver at the district garage, industrial relations appeared to take a turn for the better and a couple of the civilians agreed to collect the horse after all. Some thirty minutes later, having arrived at the location, the question then arose: how do you place a dead horse on to a low-loader? Answer: with great difficulty. Using much ingenuity and the winch, the carcase was slowly, ever so slowly, inched up the ramp. Nearly there, sighed John Blackwell. Ah, but where does one put a dead horse at nearly midnight? (Or any other time for that matter.) It was decided to deposit it in the station yard at Wharf Road, to await the arrival of the knacker later that morning.

The cortege moved away with due solemnity, sadly observed by members of the public still clutching their tufts of grass and saucers of oats. As the sad little procession threaded its way through the maze of side streets, another thought struck Blackwell: it had just been possible to crank the deceased animal up the ramp – but how does one crank it down? Dead horses will not roll! The night-duty shift at Wharf Road rallied round and with five of them taking a corner each, Dobbin lay at rest in the station yard, suitably isolated by a respectful line of 'No Parking' signs. Inspector Blackwell could not believe it; the accident happened at 5 p.m. and here he was going home for an early breakfast!

Police horses, then, are something of an anachronism.

They do have a place in law-enforcing but, like the River Police, they are really becoming more removed from modern-day policing. One thing is certain: no mounted copper would ever agree with this theory. Perhaps he is right; if police horses didn't exist, whatever would those hordes of old ladies do with their sugar lumps?

13. 'Z Cars'

Drivers of police vehicles are usually divided into five categories, from panda drivers at the bottom of the list to the drivers of Class 1 and 2 standard who drive the area-cars. These vehicles are often referred to by members of the public as 'Z Cars', after the long-running television series. Class 1 and 2 drivers are classified as 'advanced' and are permitted to drive almost all other forms of police transport.

The purpose of this segregation is to provide experience of handling progressively more powerful vehicles until one finally arrives at the three-and-a-half litre cars that are currently used for area-car work. Contrary to popular belief, these cars are not 'souped up', but rely entirely on the drivers' ability to handle them.

Even the demanding standards set by the police driving school do not ensure that all 1s and 2s are perfect; they do occasionally have accidents, as I shall later explain. It usually takes a driver a minimum of four years to reach the stage where he is even permitted to switch on the ignition in the area-car; in my own case it was nearer ten!

During these years, there are several courses at the Hendon driving school where much time is spent on both the practical and theory sides of driving. There are reaction tests, sessions on the skid-pan, bandit-chasing and written exams on both the Metropolitan Police Driving System and the Highway Code.

All these courses culminate in that momentous day of

your 'final drive', which lasts about thirty minutes. Accompanied by two examiners, you are expected to chase a 'bandit car' while conforming to the Police Driving System and the Highway Code. No matter what action the bandit car takes, you must never let yourself be drawn into an error. The bandit is usually one of the school's most experienced instructors, who leads you a merry dance.

One of the greatest difficulties for students is the requirement to give a commentary at all times whilst undergoing tests. The student has to speak out clearly and concisely on everything he can see either on, or about, the road whilst he is driving. He must mention literally every hazard, well in advance: changing road surfaces, falling leaves, sun, shadow, drains, gulleys, animals, young kids and old ladies. There are several reasons for this, the main one being that the examiners need to know not simply what you *have* seen but, much more important, what you have *not* seen.

The commentary is arguably the hardest single aspect of the whole course. Many drivers have great difficulty in getting the thing into any sort of sequence. They will often mention a junction when they are a hundred yards past it. The expression 'the traffic-lights are at red' is often indicative that they *were* at red some thirty seconds before but now they are most likely, as one tongue-tied harassed student was heard to utter, 'blue'!

After a couple of weeks, the commentary suddenly slots into place and some students become quite flamboyant: 'People on platform of bus – Could mean a 'stop' ahead – Be prepared to pull out around it – Did you see that skirt? – Traffic-lights ahead – It was half-way up her bum – They have been at green for some time – Cover brakes for possible change – Bloody hell! What a pair of knockers! – Will stop in the outside lane – They are bouncing everywhere! – Blind man on the pavement – I'm sure she ought to wear a bra! – Traffic-lights changing to amber – She's playing bloody hell with the traffic – ' It is usually at this stage that the instructor cuts in: 'Will you stop looking at the crumpet and concentrate on the road? They do not award points on the final drive for talent spotting!'

This statement will usually result in the driver lapsing into a hurt silence and the other two students in the car swivelling around to watch the 'talent' until she fades from view through the rear window.

Once the hassle of the course is over, and assuming that the student has passed all of his practical and theory exams (and only a small majority do), comes the first day actually driving the car in anger. No driver could tell you precisely what he wanted to happen on his first emergency call, but he would certainly be hoping for something really dramatic: a good meaty call with bags of drama that would cause the adrenalin to flow, perhaps with a press coverage (doubtlessly inaccurate), finally culminating in an Old Bailey appearance. On such milestones as these is the passage of area-car work inscribed.

I first took over the car at 10.45 p.m. on a quiet Monday evening. I began my required routine check of the vehicle, to be ready to leave the station by 11 p.m. I had this strange feeling of anti-climax. This evening should have been a landmark in my police career, yet I knew that it was going to be nothing of the sort. After a few years on the streets one gets to feel when the night is going to be busy or quiet and I just knew that tonight was going to be a real dead 'un.

My intuition was proved to be correct – well almost correct. If there was one call that I did not want tonight, and yet deep down was pretty sure I must get, it was the ever-recurring call to 13a Pitton Street. Almost on cue at 11.30 p.m. came our only call of that night.

'Mike Three, Mike Three. 13a Pitton Street. Disturbance. Message ends, information room 23.30 hours.'

'I bloody knew it!' I exclaimed to Derek Blake, my operator, and Bill Poulton, my plain-clothes observer. 'Wouldn't you just know that that bloody pair would be at it tonight?'

Clara and Wilfred had lived at 13a for close on twenty years and during that time the police had been called on average four times per week, although this figure did fluctuate from time to time. My personal record was three calls in one night. Their problem was fairly simple to diagnose but impossible to solve; it was sex – or rather the lack of it.

Clara's age was difficult to define but she was probably around fifty-six. She was on my short list for the ugliest woman of all time. If you were blindfolded and touched her body (heaven forbid) it would be impossible to know whether you were touching the back, front or sides. She was a complete egg on legs. She stood a little over five feet in height, weighed in at about fifteen stone and was the hairiest woman that I had ever seen. She had masses of dark hair on her head, upper lip and under her arms. Her pubic hairs, which she would display at the slightest inclination, were akin to a bedside rug. One week's night-duty at Wharf Road and all of Clara's mysteries were as a written page. Her trouble was that she liked a drink, and this always made her feel romantic. She would then turn her attention to Wilfred, her common-law husband, and this was the basis for all the hundreds of calls received from that address over the years.

Wilfred had been a former area-champion flyweight boxer but he had never been a match for Clara. He was a slight, dapper individual who probably weighed little more now than when he fought in the ring some forty years ago. He had the statutory broken nose that all former boxers sport but otherwise his whole appearance was one of an inoffensive little mouse. Clara would stagger home and grab Wilfred by his neck and begin to drag him up the stairs to their bedroom. Wilfred would struggle and squeal with all the terror of a threatened virgin and then the sparks would really fly. He was literally a battered husband. She would hit him with everything she could lift or throw. On the arrival of any police officer at the scene, the dialogue was always the same. Wilfred would rush to greet the copper with the words, 'She's sex mad, guv'nor! Bloody sex mad!'

If, in his terror, Wilfred was rash enough to step outside the front door, then Clara would immediately crash it shut, leaving poor Wilfred marooned on the pavement in whatever clothes he happened to be wearing at the time. No amount of pleading, coaxing or threatening by the police would persuade her to let him back in. The wretched man would be placed in an appalling dilemma: stand outside and freeze, or go to bed with an amorous Clara! On the other hand, this also spoke volumes for Clara's determination and tenacity; she had always claimed that in the twenty years of their 'marriage' it had never been consummated!

About once every ten days or so, Clara would be arrested for being drunk and disorderly. When this happened, she would lie down, become a dead weight and refuse to budge. The only way then to get her into the police van was for four officers each to grab a corner. If there were four, then they were fairly safe, but if there were only three, or even worse two, they were really in trouble. She would immediately pull her dress up over her head and shout, 'Wha-hey! Wha-hey!' at the top of her voice. The effect that this action had on young constables, who had never before seen a knickerless Clara, was truly amazing.

As I stopped the car outside 13a Pitton Street, the thought struck me that it had taken me ten years to become an area-car driver; surely the first night had something better in store than the sight of Clara's clitoris?

Bill Poulton knocked loudly on the battered, paint-flaked front door. All was strangely quiet from inside. Bill repeated his knocks, this time almost violently. An upstairs window opened slightly and a smiling Clara coyly popped out her hairy face.

'I had a bit of trouble with Wilfred but he's all right now – good night, boys.' So saying, she quietly closed the window.

'I'll tell you what,' said Bill. 'I think that tonight is quite an occasion. It's your first time as an area-car driver – and Wilfred has finally rung the bell! Let's celebrate and drive to Chelsea bridge for a meat pie.'

'I feel sorry for poor old Wilfred,' said Derek sadly; then his face broke into a smile. 'I bet it's the first fight of his life that he didn't come out for the second round!'

The goal that every police driver aims for is naturally the Class 1 status. It carries no extra money but it does offer a greater variety of work: sometimes six weeks in plain clothes driving a 'Q' car, possibly on a different manor; even a chance to apply for several select driving positions – with the Flying Squad, for example. The ambitious driver soon realizes, however, that once he has reached the exalted 'advance' stage he has, in effect, made a rod for his own back. The police, having spent so much money training him, are understandably reluctant to let him go to another branch of the force should he have a change of mind. Because the standard is so high, the success rate is proportionately small, therefore one can find oneself in a position of being the only area-car driver on a shift. Then it becomes a real chore. I found that I always needed to go back to walking the streets from time to time, if only to change the tempo of my life. There are few more exhausting jobs than driving an area-car non-stop in the densely populated inner city streets. I was never as tired in my pre-police job as a stone-mason as I was when driving Mike 3 from three to eleven o'clock.

Having to answer emergency calls at the height of rush-hour traffic can play havoc with one's nerve ends. Swerving for miles through endless traffic, often on the wrong side of the road, through red traffic-lights and amidst throngs of home-rushing pedestrians, to answer a 'serious disturbance' call which can turn out to be an argument over which way the door-mat should be, does not make for tranquillity. An added strain is the simple fact that area-cars are not allowed to have accidents.

The police driving school at Hendon claims that all accidents are avoidable, therefore if you are involved in one, you had just better have one hell of a good story, otherwise your fate will be an instant police driving suspension and a consideration of any road traffic offences which, in the subsequent investigation, may come to light.

Emergency calls are potentially full of jeopardy. Let me take a typical example. Brian Flood, a driving colleague of mine, was racing through Camberwell Green to a burglary call at two in the morning. The junction was partially obscured by public toilets in the centre of the road. The lights facing Brian were red but traffic in both side roads had seen, or heard, the police car and had stopped to allow it to cross. Brian slowed his speed and threaded his way through the junction. Suddenly an estate car came quickly from his right, overtaking the line of stationary vehicles that had stopped to let the police car through. The estate car then swerved between the leading stationary vehicle and the traffic-island, skidded and struck the police car amidships, slap in the centre of the junction.

You may ask what sort of driver swerves around a line of six waiting cars to cross an intersection of which he has no clear vision. A fair question, but it was Brian who was suspended for four months, it was Brian who was fined the equivalent of two weeks' wages at Lambeth Court for failing to conform to traffic-lights and driving 'without due care and attention'; and I think that few police drivers would have it any other way. They will, of course, complain about it, but to be involved in an accident dents not just their car but their pride.

By virtue of this, most area-car drivers become first-class story tellers. The unwritten law is, of course, do not have an accident. If that may be referred to as plan 'A', then plan 'B' states that if you do have an accident, you must convince the garage sergeant, who will be called upon to report it, that you in fact have not really had an accident at all. There is a great problem here, the garage sergeant will be an extremely experienced and suspicious man who has heard it all before and does not convince easily. In fact it would not be inaccurate to say that no garage sergeant in the history of the internal-combustion engine has ever believed any story ever recited to him by any policeman involved in any accident with any police car. The fact that the garage sergeant will not believe your story is almost totally irrelevant. The whole crux of the case is: can he disprove it?

I have always winced at the jocular way in which actors in any police-orientated film or TV programme blithely write off a £6000 car. Any police driver who has sustained as much as a scratch to the bodywork will know how far this piece of mythology is from the truth. This system of reporting accidents does, I feel, enrich the force. It encourages a breed of men who could explain a total wreck in such a way that one felt obliged, even duty-bound, to congratulate the driver on his ability, perhaps his mastery – some would even say artistry – at the wheel. Let us consider the exploits of one Ron Hunt.

An accident happened involving the station general-purpose car. This car was a forerunner of the panda cars and it was used for such purposes as delivering messages, ferrying personnel and supervision work. The mishap occurred at 2 a.m. when Ron skidded after taking a bend and mounted a high kerb. The damage was later estimated at £400 and in those days the cost of a new vehicle was only around £700. It was fairly obvious to Ron that any story he told the garage sergeant would have to be a real honey if he were to avoid the chop. Fortunately he was the only vehicle involved in the accident and this gave his imagination some scope – and fortune favours the brave.

The first step would have to be to change the location. Ron picked a sharp double-turn underneath a railway bridge. He then cajoled the station van driver to go to a distant expanse of railway sidings. After a brief search, a spare railway sleeper was found, hauled aboard the van and transported to the new scene of the accident. There, at the rear of a stationary lorry, it was placed at right-angles to the kerb with about a third of its length protruding from the line of the vehicle. Ron then shinned up the lamp-post and extinguished the light. It was now time to recheck his story for flaws, send for the garage sergeant and cross his fingers.

The sergeant duly arrived and Ron immediately began his story. He had swung the car, smoothly and efficiently, around the double bend; he had not used his headlights because the road was more than adequately illuminated. Unfortunately, at the crucial moment the street lamp suddenly went out. Well what could he do? Before he could take any avoiding action – ker-RASH! The garage sergeant looked at Ron in total disbelief.

'And just what the hell is a railway sleeper doing in the road, conveniently just behind a lorry which in turn is conveniently behind a street light that has in turn, conveniently gone out?'

'Vandals, sergeant?' suggested Ron helpfully.

'Vandals my arse!' exclaimed the sergeant. 'Vandals couldn't bloody lift it! Those things weigh a bloody ton!'

It was with great difficulty that Ron was able to avoid murmuring, 'I know.'

'Is that your entire bloody story then?'

'Yes, sergeant.'

There was nothing further that Ron could say that would help his cause (good crooks say very little); he had said sufficient to state his case but not enough to be nailed. He knew it and so did the sergeant. From now on it was a battle of wits but it was a battle that could only have one winner – Ron. The sergeant didn't believe the story, Ron did not expect him to, but he could not disprove it and both men knew that.

The battle of wits that is constantly waged between drivers and garage sergeants is a perfect training ground for the job itself. 'The buck' literally does stop with the area-car; there is simply nowhere else for it to go. Whatever drama takes place, whatever horror, whatever confusion, will always find itself being finally confronted by the crew of an area-car. One month's posting 'on the car', as it is usually known, will certainly find out whatever weaknesses of character a copper may have; all will be ruthlessly exposed in that month. I have seen previously inseparable friends totally unable to work with each other 'on the car'.

First, it is essential for the crew, usually a radio operator in the front and an officer in plain clothes in the back, to have implicit faith in the driver. Some crews never move past this first hurdle. If the car is roaring through traffic-lights, blind bends and over icy roads, then total confidence is an essential commodity. Nothing is worse for the driver than a nervous passenger. On the first emergency call answered by a friend of mine, his plain-clothes observer asked him to stop at the next set of traffic-lights. Just as soon as the car came to a halt, the observer leapt out, stating that he would walk back to the station and never travel on a car with him again! This action is not really conducive to the driver's confidence.

One of the most fascinating periods that I spent 'on the car' was during the late fifties. I was not yet a police driver, I was simply posted on the car as r/t operator for the month. There had been an outbreak of 'rock-an'-roll riots'. By no stretch of the imagination could any of the incidents that I saw ever be classified as 'riots' but that was the unfortunate phraseology used by most of the media at that time. A rather banal film, *Rock Around the Clock* featuring Bill Haley and his band, suddenly struck gold. Cinemas erupted into a swinging, singing, dancing, boisterous mass. There was most certainly some criminal damage but there was comparatively little violence. Although many of the rock-an'-rollers were arrested, it was usually for the two minor offences of Insulting Words or Behaviour and Obstructing Police. These offenders were usually dealt with at the courts next morning, by a two-pound fine with two weeks to pay.

As fast as we quelled the turmoil in one cinema, so we would be called to another. Police vans would rush from foyer to foyer, packed with prisoners, all of them singing, 'We're gonna rock around the clock tonight . . .'

This act would be repeated nightly for the whole of that week. By Friday, many of the cinemas found their takings had been so good that the film was held over for another week. I saw scores of arrests made during that fortnight; I never saw one policeman or rock-an'-roller assaulted, neither was I aware of any allegations made against any police officer. Times have indeed changed.

I don't know if it was the simple music played by Haley that led to the wave of 'do-it-yourself' musicians, but within a comparatively short time it was almost impossible to walk around a street corner without colliding with a skiffle-group. This in turn led to many of our local Wharf Road lads becoming 'rock stars', albeit temporarily. The local cinema, the Trocadero, was one of the three largest cinemas in Europe. Television had already made enormous inroads into its attendances; therefore in an effort to fill the massive auditorium, a series of Sunday night rock concerts was staged. Embryonic pop stars such as Cliff Richard, Tommy Steele and Marty Wilde would fill the thousands of seats on a Sunday evening in a way that no film had been able to do for years. Occasionally, the same fever that erupted during the Haley film would manifest itself in these concerts.

One problem that arose with these stage-shows was the inexperience of the 'star' to deal with any of the disturbances. Some would go totally to pieces. Others would argue with the audience. This, however, was all forgotten outside the stage-door. Here many young girls had been waiting for so long that they had not even seen the show. They were there simply to mob, scream and touch the stars as they emerged from the theatre. There was the occasional celebrity who was not treated quite so reverently, though. After a particularly heavy mobbing of a young Cliff Richard, stifled sobs could be heard emitting from a nearby deep doorway. As my eyes slowly became accustomed to the gloom, I could see a sad little screwed-up figure with green hair.

His face was buried in his hands and he kept repeating, 'Keep them away! Keep them away!' Other than myself, the nearest people were passers-by and they were taking very little notice of him. Having assured myself that I was not dealing with a leprechaun, I first thought that one of the fans was suffering from hysteria. As he lowered his hands I could see the remains of his stage make-up; I was obviously being privileged to meet one of the show's lesser stars.

'You can go home now, mate. There's hardly anyone about – and those that are aren't interested in you,' I said rather unkindly.

The fugitive lowered his hands slowly from his face and looked anxiously at me. 'Are you sure?' he said. 'Oh it's murder being a star! Can't you whisk me away in a police car; they did it for Johnny Ray,' he added plaintively.

'Sorry, mate, it's not on,' I answered softly, as if in apology for my previous harshness.

'Oh well, I suppose that I'll just have to travel by tube. I tell you, these girls are terrible, they just won't keep their hands off me!'

He wandered off towards the undergound station, looking a forlorn little chap. He was totally alone, talking to himself and believing every word of it.

The real attraction of street duty in general and area-car work in particular is, I suppose, the element of the unknown. It is one of the few occupations left in present-day society where a person can arrive for work at the beginning of their day and really have no idea at all (Clara and Wilfred excepted) what the day will bring. It could be an accident, a murder or an Irish wedding (come to think of it, I have been to Irish weddings that have been all three). It could be an armed robbery, arson or a request for directions. It could be an explosion, a false alarm or a drunk. The only certainty is the uncertainty. I suppose that's really why we do it.

14. Surely Not Guns

'Mike 3. North Peckham Road, junction of Canal Place, meet PC 923 Page. Attempted break-in and armed suspect nearby. Message ends 0230.' My stomach gave a little flutter as I wrote the short concise message into the radio log-book. In the three years that I had been a policeman, I had heard calls of a similar nature go to other cars but this would be the first time that I had been personally involved. Most 'believed armed' calls turn out to be nothing of the kind. The allegations are usually made by distressed or frightened members of the public who leap to the most dramatic of conclusions for an assortment of reasons. To some eyes, 'armed' can mean anything from catapults to umbrellas but this message stated clearly that the informant was a PC, therefore the chances were that for once the call was for real.

My driver for that month was Bill Swallow. Bill was very much a country lad, who was approaching the end of his service. He was a fairly bovine individual whose interests rarely rose beyond dog-racing. He could unravel and report the most complicated and gory road traffic accident more quickly and efficiently than anyone that I had ever worked with, but guns were most definitely not his scene. In modern parlance he would be classified as 'having no bottle'.

Bill was a 'half-a-fag man'. I never saw him smoke anything other than a cigarette butt. The small, dimly lit stub began to roll frantically from side to side of his mouth. Although smoking is not officially allowed in police vehicles, that stained, wispy inch-long roll-up was as much a part of Bill's face as his nose.

The low gears of the old Wolseley Eighteen screamed in protest as the car raced through the dark, silent Camberwell streets. Because of the lateness of the hour and the absence of traffic, I felt the quickest way to the location would simply be along the main road to Camberwell Green. From there a left turn towards Peckham that would see us at the location in around three or four minutes. Bill, on the other hand, decided to use a route of narrow streets and side roads, a route which, though shorter in distance, was longer in time. I saw him at that moment as two people: one wished to delay his arrival at the scene for as long as possible and the other, being ashamed of this attitude, was punishing the car around those tiny streets in some false spirit of daring.

We eventually arrived at the location and were greeted by a bare-headed John Page. John was a dark, curly-haired Welsh lad who looked ridiculously young without his helmet. North Peckham and Canal Place is a location that is not strictly on the Wharf Road manor but the Peckham car crew were in at their own station for their meal break and Mike 3 was covering both areas. I knew John slightly because we both played football for the division and we had in fact played together the previous afternoon.

'Wassamatter, Taff, lad?' I asked.

'There's a bloke in there somewhere and the bastard's just shot me.'

Blood covered his right wrist and was running freely down the truncheon that he held at his side.

John had apparently stumbled on two men breaking into a shop. On seeing him, each man ran off in opposite directions. John set off in pursuit of one of them. The suspect had made off towards an old tenement block that backed on to the rear of a row of seedy Victorian terraced houses. John was an extremely fit individual and easily gained on his man. When the distance between the two had closed to about four yards, the suspect stopped abruptly and turned. For the first time John could see that he held a pistol in his hand. Two shots were fired and John looked down at the burning sensation that he felt in his right arm. When he looked up again, the suspect had vanished. By the time that John had found the telephone box to call for assistance, his assailant could have been miles away.

I looked up at the tenement; it was six storeys high, there were four flats to each floor, and there were eight block entrances. There must have been close on two hundred dwellings in that block and the suspect could have been in any one of them, if indeed he was still in the area at all!

Bill Swallow returned to the car to radio for assistance (as I knew he would) and I began to search the block. There did not seem to be any point in banging on random doors, so I simply climbed the dimly lit stairs up to the roof. Access to this part of the building was easily gained via an old broken door and I walked across to the low parapet and looked down at the street below. I could hear the first of the police cars in the distance. The roar of their engines cut easily through the quiet night air.

I suddenly realized my own vulnerability. In company with most of my colleagues, my police issue torch did not work; but also it was my habit to leave my truncheon under the seat of the car – and that was exactly where it was at that precise moment. I was too furious with myself to be frightened. Of all the daft situations to be in. If anything did happen, I not only wouldn't be able to see it – but I wouldn't be able to hit it!

I decided to carry on searching the roof, mainly because

there was very little cover, and within a couple of minutes I had covered the whole roof-top. I gave a final glance over the parapet before I descended the stairs and in the distance I could see the ambulance approaching, presumably to convey Taff Page to hospital.

When I was half-way down the staircase, I could hear the sound of footsteps rushing up towards me. Two coppers with truncheons drawn came into view.

'He's on the roof!' they panted.

'He's not,' I answered.

'We've just seen him, looking over the edge.'

'You saw me!' I exclaimed.

Ignoring me, they brushed angrily past and continued on their pointless journey skywards.

As I neared the ground, through the window on each landing I could see about a dozen coppers clumping all over the place and duplicating each other's work. At least two of them appeared to be running around in circles – I was not impressed.

'Let's get some bloody order here,' said a stout old bespectacled constable. He had just begun to reorganize the chaos when I noticed a large broken window on the first landing of the staircase. I had been so intent on rushing to the roof – as no doubt were the two lads that I had met on the staircase – that I did not notice it on my original entry into the block.

I looked through the gap in the glass and there were several segments of clothing attached to its sharp edges. The window led on to a small shed that stood at the end of the rear garden of one of the Victorian houses from the next street. I climbed through and eventually dropped down into a back garden. The problem that I now had was that the only light came from the fortunately bright stars. I stood still for a moment to enable my eyes to become accustomed to the gloom and then I attempted to open the shed door. I could not move it; it was securely padlocked from outside. I moved around the neglected plot, feeling into and behind bushes, and my hand closed over a stout wooden stake that had originally been tethered to a now long-dead plant. I snapped it off at ground level, to use in lieu of a truncheon, and resumed my blind groping.

Looming up in front of me, I could gradually make out a small brick out-house with a wooden latched door; it was an outside toilet. I lifted the latch and slowly opened the door. My left hand tightened around my stake. The lavatory was pitch dark and as I searched blindly with my right hand, I first felt the toilet-paper holder, then the cistern chain and finally the down pipe – empty! Stepping back into the night air, I breathed a sigh of relief and secured the door.

I was suddenly aware of the sound of shoes scraping against a hard surface. Gradually a curly head appeared from over the wall of the next garden. I could see that the newcomer was not in uniform and I could also see what looked very much like a gun in his hand. I stood motionless for a second, then I slowly eased my left arm back in order to wallop the head with a fearsome and stunning blow. A beam of light struck me between the eyes.

'Who the hell are you?' said a rough cockney voice.

'Put that bloody torch out, you're blinding me!' I snapped irritably.

'You idiot! I nearly shot you!' said the head.

By pure coincidence, two cars, each containing four members of the Flying Squad, had been returning from an ambush that had not transpired. It was believed that the suspects in their anticipated raid would be armed, therefore the squad themselves had drawn weapons. As they were returning to Scotland Yard, they had heard of John Page's shooting from over the car radio and had in fact been the second car on the scene.

A large bulky body followed the head over the wall until a giant of a man about six feet six inches in height dropped down alongside me.

'What's in 'ere?' he said, as he walked towards the toilet.

'It's a lavatory. I've been in there and it's empty,' I pointed out.

He lifted the latch and pushed open the door. It opened for a distance of about eighteen inches, then it crashed shut almost trapping his fingers.

'I thought you said it was bloody empty?' he yelled. 'There's some bastard in there!'

'Well they must have been sitting on the floor,' I said apologetically

'Oh, don't that count then?' he snapped, with heavy sarcasm.

We heard the door bolt slam shut.

My new-found colleague crashed his huge body against the door but it failed to have any effect.

'Hang on, we'll do it together,' I said, anxiously trying to get back into favour.

We leaned back in order to get the same momentum. Suddenly there was a loud bang.

'The bastard's shooting at us,' he yelled.

The noise drew every copper from all over the location and soon about a dozen of us were gathered outside the lavatory door for a council of war.

'Are you going to come out with your 'ands up, or do you want to be shot in a shit-'ouse?' called out the detective with the gun.

There was no reply. One PC climbed on to the roof and began to remove the slates.

'Can we break the door down with this?' said a uniformed figure picking up a heavy oak fence-post.

Four of us secured some sort of hold on it and, holding

it like a battering ram, we charged the door. The third charge went clean through the centre plank and there was a scream of pain as the end of our ram pinned whoever was inside the privvy against the back wall.

The door was rapidly ripped from its hinges as men thrust their hands inside to grab the gunman. Eventually a white-faced fellow of about twenty years was dragged unceremoniously from the lavatory. He kept repeating, 'I'm sorry! I'm sorry!'

'You're only sorry 'cos you've been caught, you bastard,' snarled the detective.

As the gunman was led away to the waiting police van, I looked again at the lavatory. I was almost totally destroyed, the door and frame were smashed to pieces and most of the roof was missing.

People were silhouetted against scores of lighted windows; they seemed disappointed that they were not going to witness an early-morning shoot-out. Shapeless winceyette nightdresses were topped by gaping, toothless mouths that were in turn crowned by tiaras of wire hair curlers. Rounded whale-like beer bellies peeped obscenely through buttonless pyjamas. The blue stubbled chins could be seen, or perhaps easily imagined, even in that poor light. Strangely, the only house that did not sport an audience was the one in whose garden the drama had taken place. I called up to the bedroom window next door.

'Where are they, luv? Away?'

'Nah, mate,' answered a round, turban-headed face. 'They're stone deaf. They carn't 'ear nuffink.'

'Well haven't they got a surprise in the morning,' I thought. When the first of them emerge for their early-morning wee, he or she is going to find his lavatory demolished!

I decided to spend some time prowling around the

scene of the incident – all sorts of fascinating items can turn up once the hue and cry has abated. Who knows, I might even have found a torch that worked. I traced John Page's route from the shop doorway to the tenement block. Whilst still a few yards away from the block entrance, I saw a dark round object rocking ever so gently in the quiet night breeze. It was John's helmet. I picked it up by its strap and began to brush off the dust and pavement grit. I saw what I first took to be a small round stain on each side of the helmet. I tried to flick it off with my fingernail but my forefinger went straight through the 'stain'. A bullet had entered one side of the helmet and emerged through the opposite side, doing little more damage to Taff than ruffling his normally well-tousled hair.

I walked back to the area-car, where Bill Swallow sat behind the steering wheel with the engine quietly ticking over. The thought struck me that from the moment Bill had called for assistance, he had remained in the car ever since. I tossed the helmet into the back seat and before I could recite to him the story of the night's happenings, a small Hillman saloon car swung dramatically around the corner and screeched to a halt. The passenger, a tall uniformed PC, leapt out and ran swiftly across the road towards us. I wound down my window expectantly. The tall policeman slipped his hand into his jacket and I found myself staring into a rather dangerous-looking revolver.

'I'm the authorized shot, mate; you've got a suspect holed up with a gun somewhere?'

'Well by now I should think he is holed up in the first cell in Peckham nick. Where'd you come from – Tombstone?' I asked rather sarcastically.

'You didn't have anyone authorized on your division, so they whistled me over from Bethnal Green.'

'Well you'd better just whistle back over again, 'cos he's nicked.'

'Okay, mate, see yer, ta-ta,' he said cheerily. With that, he ran back across the road and slipped quickly into the car and within seconds, it had roared away.

That was the system that operated in the Metropolitan Police up until the late 1960s. There were just a few 'authorized shots' at each station and if at any shooting incident, either real or imaginary, none of these men were on duty, then a 'shot' would have to be obtained from wherever else one could be quickly found. The training of these men was as slip-shod as their distribution. An officer would not be considered for training until he had been at a station for some years. The trouble with this system was that the time chosen for training was at a period of a man's service in which he had become a little restless anyway. Perhaps he would be thinking about trying for another branch of the force, or wishing to sit the promotion exam. The result was that it would be rare at any shooting incident for any authorized shot to be present in under thirty minutes and often it would be nearer an hour. This could obviously seem like eternity (in every sense of the word) if one was pinned down by some nutter who thought he was Billy the Kid.

In 1961 I drove a van-load of these official authorized shots to an underground rifle range in north London for a periodic refresher course. At the end of their session, each would put a couple of shillings in a hat and the best shot would pocket the money. Because one of the number was required at court that morning, I was invited to take part unofficially in the shoot-off. I had been a reasonably good shot in the army but I had never fired a pistol in my life. In spite of this handicap, I won the 'kitty'. Instead of being pleased about this, I was in fact seriously alarmed. One man in particular would line up his sight, adopt the correct stance and appear to be totally relaxed. He would then gently squeeze the trigger – just after he had closed both his eyes and turned his head!

In the middle of the sixties, violent crime had begun to escalate and the Wharf Road CID received information that a leading member of a gang that had been responsible for a large number of armed robberies was hiding up in a Camberwell flat. The informant further alleged that the suspect was not only armed but would not hesitate to use his gun. The flat in question was in a big rambling old house that was let off into separate rooms. Unfortunately, the informant could not assist with the exact location of our crook's room.

I was the driver of 'Mike 3' that month.. My operator was Alan Martin, a big amiable Londoner. Alan was on the list of authorized shots. The plan was that two armed CID officers would enter the front door and search the top half of the house while Alan and I would enter by the back door and search the bottom half.

I drove to the meeting point, nervously aware that I was going to be the only one of the four who would not be armed. I parked at the corner of Camberwell Church Street for a few minutes. Alan spent the time usefully by giving himself a crash course in familiarization of the pistol that he had just drawn from the station safe.

'Where's the safety catch on these things then?' he casually asked.

'Look, mate,' I said, desperately trying to maintain an outward calm. 'When we go into that house, no matter what happens, *never* be behind me. It's going to be bad enough with that bastard firing at my front without you shoving bullets up my arse.'

We were soon joined by the CID and exactly on cue the

four of us broke into the two separate entrances. The truest words that Shakespeare ever wrote were, 'cowards die many times'. Every time we smashed our way through a locked door, I died a little. We finally kicked our way into no fewer than eight rooms and in each of them I winced and cowered behind Alan's broad back, but each room was completely empty. As we climbed the stairs to the top half of the house, we were met by the suspect and the two CID officers coming down. Actually our villain was quite a let-down, I have rarely seen such an insignificant-looking crook. Although the fact that he had been shacked up there with some other prisoner's wife for two weeks probably did little to help his appearance. He did, however, lose a certain amount of this insignificance when he was searched and was found to have in his possession a revolver and a couple of thousand pounds in cash.

It was shortly after this incident that the whole concept of the use of police guns began to change. Up until the late sixties, the system for dealing with a crime in which firearms had been used was totally inadequate. However, the sharp escalation of violent crime during that period made it essential that improvements were made in the standards of authorized shots. Also improved was the distribution of these men. Their numbers did not greatly increase but their availability certainly did. No more did the reply come back, after an urgent appeal for a gun, 'Sorry, mate. Our authorized shot's on holiday!'

In almost every incident during that period where guns had been used to commit a crime, if the villain was caught at all, then it was solely through the bravery, obstinacy, cussedness or just plain stupidity of some policeman or member of the public. There was no master scheme for dealing with firearms, except that most coppers felt that they had been classified by society as expendable. For ten years I drove an area-car in one of the highest crime areas in London, yet never once during that time was I ever given one word of instruction on what action to take in a situation where firearms were used.

This eleventh-hour overhaul of our firearms code really paid off in some of the more dramatic sieges of the times. If either the Balcombe Street or Spaghetti House sieges had taken place a few years earlier, the police would have had to depend on the co-operation of the bandits to keep the whole thing going until an authorized shot could be whistled over from Bethnal Green.

The one big flaw in this reorganization is the fact that firearms are still kept under lock and key in the local police station. This really cannot be avoided. But this system does of course leave the vulnerable period, between the time that the need for a gun arises and the time when that need can be met. The whole developing situation will have its foundation there. Whether blood is subsequently shed, whether lives are eventually lost, will almost certainly be determined in those first few minutes. It is also in those vital minutes when a stupid action can be disastrous, an intelligent action commendable, and a courageous action breathtaking. The latter course was taken by a good friend of mine, Bill Kinniburgh.

Bill is a slim, quietly spoken Scot, reluctantly nudging early middle age. He also happened to be the driver of Mike 3 on the day that it picked up the trail of a stolen motor car, the occupant of which was strongly averse to being arrested. Having broadsided from Camberwell Road into New Church Road, the bandit car was finally forced to stop by the pursuing police car. The occupant leapt from the vehicle and pointed a pistol at Bill and the two other members of Mike 3. Each of the three policemen faltered slightly, whilst waiting for the next stage of the game to develop. All three slowly resumed their moves towards the gunman who took deliberate aim and fired. This seemed to incense Bill. He neither ducked nor dived but strode briskly up to the bandit and demanded the pistol.

'Give us the gun, Jimmy!' Jimmy did.

A very simple action, all over in a few minutes. But sometimes I wonder if even those of us who work with such people ever really stop to think exactly what sort of person is capable of this brand of courage. Bill gambled entirely on the force of his own presence to remove the gun from an unknown crook – a crook, I might add, who had already shown his willingness to shoot. There is no margin for error – you are either very right or 'dead' wrong. Even in an unequal physical struggle, one is always in with some sort of a chance, but to walk up unarmed to a trapped gunman who has already fired at you and then demand his gun is something pretty special. It should be said that Bill is a born gambler; if you knew the amount of times his horse selections had let him down, it may be easier to understand why he took such a gamble with his own life. Following the dictum, 'You win a few, you lose a few', he probably thought he was due for a winner anyway. Bill's action won him the Queen's Police Medal for Gallantry – but it lost him the next five races at Sandown Park.

Some weeks later, during the early hours of the morning, Lou Peters, a friend of both Bill and me, disturbed a man breaking into a shop in the Wharf Road. It is a fact of life that when there has been an incident on the manor involving a gun, a policeman will be subconsciously aware of that fact for some months. At the back of his mind will be the thought, 'Will this shadowy figure turn and pull a gun on me? If so, how will I react? More importantly, how will *he* react? Will he shoot me? Will I be badly injured? Will I be very dead?' All of these thoughts race through your mind in such a situation.

When the suspect ran from the shop, Lou instinctively flinched, but within a couple of seconds he realized that the burglar was more afraid of him than he was of the burglar. Lou had therefore got his first priority right; now he must work on the second one, i.e. the capture of the crook. Even Lou's greatest admirers will never claim that he is an athlete, and the suspect was opening up quite a gap between them. However, if Lou's original thought had been that the suspect may be armed, why could not the same thought be planted in the mind of the suspect?

In his best 'Starsky and Hutch' American, Lou called out, 'Freeze! Or I'll shoot!'

The effect was magic. The man not only stopped running but dived to the ground with his arms and legs outstretched and burst into tears! The effect on the poor bloke was so staggering that Lou didn't have the heart to tell him that he wasn't armed at all. Right to this day, there is a furtive little Wharf Road villain who believes, contrary to the accepted national practice, that all local coppers not only carry six-shooters but will blast your innards out after just one warning. Nobody is going to convince him that the police aren't armed.

15. Community Copper

Early in 1969, I was sent for by the superintendent.

'There's a whole new aspect of policing beginning; I just wondered, perhaps, if you might like to get in on the ground floor,' he said, matter-of-factly.

'What actually is it?' I asked suspiciously. Experience had taught me that if you are offered a different job anywhere in the police force it is usually to your detriment.

'It's called "home-beating". You'll be a sort of community cop. You'll police just one small area all of the time and come rain or shine – that will be your patch. I suppose it's really something similar to the old village system,' he explained.

'Well if it's a village system, it's hardly new, then, guv'nor, is it? If I'm going back to walking the streets full-time, what advantages do I gain – and why am I the only bloke at the station to be offered the job?' I asked distrustfully.

'Well the first advantage is that there is no night-duty.' (He need not have gone on any longer, he'd sold the idea to me in that sentence alone, but I was determined to play hard to get.) 'Secondly, at least up to a point, you will be a free agent. We will just turn you loose and you will be left free to work your forty-eight hours a week, in whatever way you see fit, depending of course on the requirements of your patch. And thirdly, you are by no means unique. You are the only one offered the job at this station because it is in the nature of an experiment. We will give it a few weeks' trial and if it works, we will extend the system to cover the whole of the Wharf Road manor. If it doesn't work, you'll be back on night-duty within a month,' he said pointedly.

It seemed to me at this stage that I was losing the battle. In my dislike of night-duty he not only had a key card, he knew exactly when to play it.

'What are my job requirements?' I asked the question more to buy time than out of any desire for community policing knowledge.

'Why do people always ask "what are my job requirements?" when they can't think of anything else to say? Look,' he said, with just a touch of vinegar in his voice, 'do you want this job or not? Yes or no?'

'Can I try it for a month, guv'nor?'

'Done! Come back and see me in a month and we'll talk about it again, okay?' So saying, he rose from his desk to indicate to me that the audience was at an end.

'You still have not told me my job requirements, sir,' I added, a little defensively.

'Frankly, I don't know them. You will obviously have to get to know the community, probably by going into schools, youth clubs, shops and tenant associations and such like, but in the main it will be left to you. You have been at this station for the last seventeen years, so you appear to be settled here. I have no desire to offer this sort of job to anyone who has set his sights on some other department, or perhaps anyone who wishes to sit the promotion exam. You were born locally, your family live locally, and you think and act like a local person. My field of choice was so limited, that I suppose you seemed the only man suited,' he said blandly.

'Thanks, guv'nor, that's made me feel really good. It's just about the best description of "PC Plod" that ever I've heard – but I'll give it a try anyway.'

At 7 a.m. on the following Monday morning, I parked the night-duty Mike 3 in the car-bay at Wharf Road for the last time. I scurried quickly home in order to snatch a quick four hours' sleep before I reported back at 2 p.m. that afternoon for my first day as a home-beat constable.

The whole theory of home-beating in the Metropolitan Police ran counter to all previously accepted standards of police discipline. It had long been an offence for a policeman even to enter a shop on duty in order to make a private purchase. A friend of mine once spent half an hour in the superintendent's office after purchasing a tuppenny tap washer. Yet now it was clearly force policy actively to encourage an officer if not to make purchases then most certainly to frequent the shops where he may easily do so. Hours of work were also rigidly adhered to, yet I was now being told that my hours would be so flexible that I almost felt that I was self-employed.

Over the years, in the constant battle of wits between a PC and his supervising officers, an unwritten code of practice had evolved. Both sides knew the game. They had, after all, one thing in common: they were all, or at least had been, street constables themselves. With the new-found freedom, all the challenge seemed to have disappeared. It just wouldn't seem the same when I entered the butcher's, baker's, confectioner's, grocer's, barber's and telephone box not to check that an inspector or a section sergeant would collide with me at the door. As I wandered out on to those familiar old streets, they suddenly took on a new air of interest – and isolation.

I had decided which would be my best approach to my 'parishioners'. I knew both the area and the people who lived there well enough to know that if I rushed around knocking on doors or stopping people in the streets it would have a reverse effect to any community coppering that I may have in mind. My approach had to be made on a slow, developing, here-I-am-if-you-want-me basis. It was not going to be easy.

Within a few weeks, a whole different world opened up to me. The array of questions I was asked and problems I was presented with were staggering. I began to have the feeling that there were whole families in the Wharf Road area whose entire life has been geared to my arrival on the home beat. I was asked about holidays, treatment for budgies, wallpapering, social security, conservation, contraception, politics and prison visits. I was called upon to chastise drunken husbands (occasional success), errant wives (hundred per cent failure), wayward kids and obstinate grandparents. I fixed curtain rails (terribly), tap-washers and door-bells (even worse); I tried, oh how I tried, to avoid giving advice on cars. (I am the world's worst mechanic.) I wrote letters for people who couldn't write, made telephone calls for people who couldn't use the telephone, I traced lost kids, lost parents and lost grandparents (the greatest success here was a mother who had been missing for thirty-one years!). I received anonymous threatening letters (I recognized the writing), anonymous threatening phone calls (I recognized the voice), and an anonymous cake with forty candles on it for my fortieth birthday (it was stale). I was invited to christenings, weddings and divorces (often in that order, particularly with the very young), I received letters of thanks and an allegation of theft. (This was from a very confused old lady who believed that I had stolen two shoe-horns. The two months that I waited for the Director of Public Prosecutions to state that there was no evidence did not help. The deputation of local people who insisted on seeing my divisional commander were, however, a great comfort.) In short, every day on the home beat could be different; it could also be great fun.

*

Possibly the most rewarding side of community policing are the school visits. These are essential if a policeman really wishes to become known in his neighbourhood. Children always assume that if you enter their schools from time to time, then you will be as familiar with their face as they are with yours. This can work very much to an advantage if a child is committing some distant mischief. The merest sight of a copper will often cause most kids to be long-gone before any face-to-face action can take place. This is not usually so with the appearance of the local home-beat cop. A very loud and prolonged 'OY! Come here!' can work wonders.

Often children will walk by in company with their parents. As they approach they tend to look a little bashful, but as soon as they are a few yards past, one can usually hear a stage whisper that will carry for three streets: 'That's our copper who comes in our school.' Not all local children, of course, attend local schools. Those who do will often trot up to me with the obvious intention of impressing their less parochial friends. I was in attendance on a neighbourhood festival when a girl aged about eight engaged me in conversation. The young boy accompanying her was obviously expected to be impressed, although I had the feeling that he was anything but. After a few minutes' conversation, she left to enjoy one of the many side-shows.

'Who's that?' said the lad, showing just mild curiosity.

'That's PC Cole and he goes to my school,' said the girl condescendingly.

'Dahn't believe yer,' responded her doubting companion.

'He does, I tell you!' said the girl, raising her voice indignantly.

The boy looked at me disbelievingly for a few moments, then he turned to her and with a smug expression upon his face said, 'All right then, what year is he in?'

It is very easy for a policeman to delude himself on the impact that he is making on children in schools. They may of course be genuinely glad to see him. On the other hand, he may be simply a break from the seemingly endless school lessons. As such, he may receive a welcome out of all proportion to his contribution. A two-minute standing ovation after showing a ten-minute film on police dogs does seem to me to hint more of a missed lesson on maths than of any particular stage magnetism that I may personally radiate. Because of this danger, it is always a good feeling when one occasionally sees tangible proof of the power of such visits. I have always tended to use any such example, to enable me to stress other points that I may wish to make. Even this policy can kick-back, as happened on a visit to a junior school to show a road safety film.

I arrived outside John Ruskin Street School, where I was due to spend some twenty minutes with six infant classes in the assembly hall. While I was locking my car, I saw a girl aged about ten and her younger brother aged about six running along the pavement on the opposite side of the road. They were obviously very late and I lingered to watch them cross the road. I was convinced that they would forget all of their training and rush across – a factor that I would bring out in my preliminary talk.

To my astonishment, they stopped exactly opposite the school entrance and the girl then walked carefully from behind a dangerously parked lorry, looked both ways and then crossed the road and disappeared into the school. Although I was quite impressed with the girl, the boy was about to astound me. He did not seem at all concerned that his sister had forsaken him. He calmly walked further along the pavement to a part of the road that was free from parked vehicles, did his road drill beautifully and walked smartly across the road and into the school. I swelled with pride – at last I was getting through, my words were not falling on stony ground after all. I would hold that child up at assembly as an example to be emulated by all safety-conscious children.

Later, after showing the film and while the children were still seated in the hall, I walked over to this likeable child and I smiled benignly.

'What is your name, young man?' I requested.

'David, sir,' came the quiet reply.

'Well, David, I was watching you when you came into school this morning and I was most impressed by the way in which you followed your road drill. Stand up so that everyone in the hall can see you.' Now I should have ended the interview right there while I was ahead, but no, not me, I just have to overplay my hand. 'Now, David, tell all the boys and girls just why we do not cross the road from behind parked lorries.' I stepped back modestly to allow this young cherub to say how PC Cole had completely influenced his thinking when it came to road safety.

David cleared his throat, wiped his nose on the cuff of his shirt and said in a loud voice: 'We do not cross the road from behind parked lorries 'cos they might 'ave a bomb in 'em.'

The local copper is of course quite handy for schools to use as an impartial agent, for example, drawing raffle prizes for the PTA and judging races on the school sports day. Except for the fact that it always rains on sports days, neither of these tasks are particularly demanding. There is one such task, however, that really fills me with dread. At no other time in my police service have I experienced the feeling of impending gloom that manifests itself when I am asked to 'do a little competition judging'. Now I don't mind Easter bonnets, or the occasional dirty-fingered cake; what really fills me with foreboding is the school talent contest.

'Our Friday lunches are our speciality. If you care to come to lunch on that day, perhaps you could do a little competition judging?' said the headmistress, somewhat deviously I felt.

'Well,' I said, viewing the prospect of a school dinner with violent apathy, 'perhaps I'll call in after lunch.'

She would not hear of it, however, and somewhat apprehensively I arrived for my egg salad and syrup pud. Contrary to my fears, the meal was excellent and so I was in a pleasant frame of mind when a short time later the whole junior school trooped into the assembly hall. Up until that moment, I'd had no idea what I was supposed to be judging. It was a few days before the Easter holiday and I assumed I would be expected to pass my expert eye over a few bonnets and make a couple of passing references to road safety. I was shown to a table at the side of a stage and given a long list of names. Suddenly it dawned on me: I had agreed to judge the talent acts, FOOL!

I was absolutely panic-stricken and frantically sought a way out. Too late, the hall floor was full of expectant kids and the seats at the sides were full of expectant mums, all no doubt confident that their child would win the first prize – an eight-ounce bar of chocolate.

'How many acts do we have?' I weakly asked my fellow judges (the school secretary and the cook).

'Forty-three,' replied the school secretary wearily, obviously having been through the whole thing many times before.

'Forty-three!' I screamed in sheer disbelief.

'Yes, but don't worry,' said the cook, 'there are always some who are far too sick to take part.'

What did she mean, 'too sick to take part'? I had also

eaten that syrup pudding!

I glanced down at the list, which gave the name of each child together with his or her intentions. E.g. Freddy Hall – Jokes, Mandy Davis – Acrobat. There was also a space on the list for comments. I could think of a few and we hadn't even started.

We were soon under way with a plump, seven-year-old 'Frank Spenser'. I did not realize at that moment that out of forty-three acts, twelve were going to be Frank Spensers! It seemed that every other act began with ''Ullo Bettee.' I marked each act out of one hundred. My favourite was George, number thirty-six. He was introduced by his teacher thus: 'The next act is George and he is going to sing "My ding-a-ling".' There followed an embarrassing silence. No George. The teacher cleared her throat, 'I'm sorry, George will not be appearing, he has gone to the lavatory.' I gave him a hundred marks for his brevity.

Mandy then entered stage left for her acrobatics. She was a fat little five-year-old fairy, her hair in bunches and her leotard in holes. She went head-over-heels and fell sideways. She then stood up, faced the audience, curtsied beautifully and said in a sweet little voice, 'I can't do any more. Bye-bye.' Her act, which took just eight seconds longer than the absent George's, qualified her for ninety-two marks on my list. We then had four more Frank Spensers and, finally, six-year-old Billy told a joke that I hoped to God he didn't understand and the show was over. I was so punch-drunk at that moment that I would have voted Streisand and Sinatra a miss.

My vote for the absent George was over-ruled by my two colleagues and Janet won with her recitation on daffodils which at five minutes I thought was an hour too long. The headmistress later explained that Janet was the grand-daughter of the cook – and the cook was rather temperamental. Because of the importance of a good cook to any junior school, I readily subscribed my vote to this blatant nepotism and Janet duly collected her now melting chocolate bar. In spite of this somewhat bent diplomatic decision, I had to agree inwardly with the thoughts offered by Barbara, a cheeky-faced cockney kid sitting in the front row of the hall, who said in a loud whisper, 'Cor! I fink that's a right bleedin' swiz.'

Schools, of course, form only a part of any home-beat officer's job. One of the never-ending tasks is dealing with the aptly named 'problem families'. Very often trouble will erupt between such families and their more orthodox neighbours. I feel enormous sympathy for people who live next door to, or even near such families. Their lives and nerves can be disrupted in a way which more detached people, however well-intentioned, can never understand.

A real classic 'problem family' was the O'Sheas. The family consisted of Mrs Peggy O'Shea and her nine children. In all of the years that I knew them, I never once saw the husband. Local rumour had it that he popped home every year or so to put Peggy in the family way, then left a few days later.

A whole string of social workers had cut their teeth on the O'Sheas. Just occasionally, a good rapport would emerge between the family and one of these workers, but the very high turnover of social workers in the borough made it almost inevitable that the O'Sheas should take one step forward and two steps back.

The thieving committed by this family was enormous. They would nick anything they could lift and if they couldn't lift it singly, then they would lift it collectively. However they rarely took any of this swag home. Too many official-sounding people wandered in and out of 54 Freeze House for Peggy's peace of mind. What with social workers, community workers, DHSS representatives, housing welfare officers, debt collectors, irate neighbours and coppers, 'Well a woman's got no place to call her own, 'as she, Mr Cole?' she once said to me.

The main problem posed by a family like the O'Sheas lay in the difference between their way of life and that of their neighbours. They did not go to school, nor did they go to work. Therefore they were not governed by the same 'checks and balances' that were the lot of other people nearby. A knock on their door late at night would probably find the whole family still up. A late morning call would find them all in bed. Therefore noise became a monster. The bare wooden floorboards would reverberate with every running child's footsteps throughout the entire block. Authority has never *begun* to come to terms with families like the O'Sheas. In order to placate neighbours, the family is moved on every few years. Another reason for this action is to allow routine maintenance work in the flat itself. Council workers will not enter any of their rooms unless fumigated first.

Yet the O'Sheas rarely seem unhappy. They have a family spirit which I have seldom seen equalled. The children think the world of Peggy and have a great feeling of loyalty for each other. They are usually, with the exception of a few sores, in surprisingly good health. They are dirty, cunning, devious and thoroughly likeable. Peggy never once failed to make me smile.

I wandered into a block of flats one Saturday evening after reports that twelve mats had vanished from outside front doors. These mats only seemed to disappear on a Saturday. A few minutes before ten o'clock, I saw nine-year-old Peter O'Shea furtively enter the flats via the emergency staircase. I intended stopping him when he left the block – in almost certain possession of the goods. Peter was under ten and therefore classified in law as below the age of criminal responsibility, a fact which Peggy drummed into all her children (especially six-year-old Frankie, who was the family expert at stealing from cars).

A couple of minutes after he had entered the block, Peter was being led out again by a rather irate-looking gentleman clasping Peter's left ear. On seeing me, the man called out, 'This little sod has been in here for the last three Saturday nights nicking door-mats. I've been waiting for him tonight and sure enough, the little sod has come back.'

'Did you see him take any mats, or anything else for that matter?' I asked.

'No. But it's got to be him, 'cos he's a right little tea-leaf [thief].'

'Well . . . I'm afraid that there's no real evidence of theft . . .' I said thoughtfully, prolonging the conversation as much as possible because the man still held Peter's ear. 'But give him to me anyway. I know his mum. She can come down to the station to collect him.'

'I'm only nine!' yelled Peter quickly.

'I know,' I replied, 'and I'm taking you down to Wharf Road Police Station for your own protection. A nice little chappie like you shouldn't be wandering around a place like this at this time of night, in the dark as well! Tut tut. Anything might happen to you.' Taking hold of Peter's right ear, I walked him back to the nick.

During the ten-minute walk back to the station, my attention was drawn by a young female voice calling my name. I turned to see fifteen-year-old Jean O'Shea running to catch up with us.

'Hullo, Jean. What can I do for you?' I asked.

'You've nicked Peter!' she exclaimed.

'Now would I do a thing like that? I'm just taking him down to the station to wait for your mum to collect him. You can save me a journey, perhaps you'll tell your mum for me?' Just as if she wouldn't! The news of Peter's apprehension would be on the O'Shea's grapevine quicker than radio.

Some fifteen minutes later I was talking to Peter in the interview room at Wharf Road. He had turned out his pockets and among his possessions were ten American dollars. My first reaction was that he had sold his sister, but then I remembered that I had just spoken to her.

'Where did you get this money from, Peter?' I asked, more out of curiosity than anything else.

'I save foreign coins,' said Peter.

'Did you save them from some Yank's pocket, then?' I said cuttingly.

'Em — er, a-posh-American-gave-them-to-me-for-running-errands,' he recited at breakneck speed.

I decided that it was time for a little obnoxiousness on my part. I moved closer to the boy and wagged my finger just under his nose. 'Look here, you lying little sod — ' Suddenly the door opened and Peggy O'Shea, followed by at least three of her brood, walked in and smiled at me benignly.

'Oooooh look!' she said, turning to her kids. 'It's that nice PC Cole who teaches you how to cross the road, say "Hullo" to him nicely, then.'

'Hullo, PC Cole,' chorused the trio.

There's one thing that can be said about me, I know when I'm beaten.

'Sign for this bloody kid and his money, Peggy, then you can all go home,' I said wearily.

Peggy signed.

'Good night, PC Cole,' they all chirrupped, as the kids skipped gaily out into the night.

'They seemed a nice family,' said a young PC who was trying to walk a rubbery-legged drunk into the charge-room.

'Oh they are, they are,' said the station officer, raising his eyes to heaven.

School kids and problem families do not, of course, constitute the entire repertoire of an urban copper's work, although they can typify it. Unfortunately the trend of the last few years is for a man to spend less and less time on his patch. The enormous increase in large-scale policing at such events as demonstrations and football matches, and the security obviously needed for the many visits by foreign leaders, all take a heavy toll of the available manpower, as do the special squads to combat the great increases in street crime. All of the gaps caused by the creation of any such squads are to be plugged. It is possible that during a holiday period, for example, a man could be working as much away from his station as at it. Sometimes one feels little more than a static reserve pool for a mobile and ever-changing street problem.

Some men develop an affinity for their home beats. No matter how grotty the area may seem, that is the part of London to which he feels he really belongs. I have lived in Lewisham, which is some miles away from my home beat, for the last twenty years; but it is in Southwark where I feel most at home. I feel no more than a temporary visitor to the Lewisham streets, yet the streets of Southwark are like a pair of old shoes to me; they may not look very smart, but my God how they fit.

The bodies, dogs, demos, drunks and fights; the villains and the victims; the brutal, the gentle, the cowardly and the brave; the haters, the lovers and the just plain indifferent . . . One day I shall have to live without them; it won't be easy. As my grandmother used to say, 'It's better than walking the streets.'

Fontana Paperbacks: Non-fiction

Fontana is a leading paperback publisher of non-fiction. Below are some recent titles.

- ☐ POLICEMAN'S LOT Harry Cole £2.95
- ☐ POLICEMAN'S PATROL Harry Cole £2.95
- ☐ POLICEMAN'S PROGRESS Harry Cole £2.95
- ☐ POLICEMAN'S PRELUDE Harry Cole £2.95
- ☐ POLICEMAN'S STORY Harry Cole £2.95
- ☐ POLICEMAN'S PATCH Harry Cole £2.95
- ☐ POLICEMAN'S GAZETTE Harry Cole £2.95
- ☐ VET FOR ALL SEASONS Hugh Lasgarn £2.95
- ☐ IMPRESSIONS OF MY LIFE Mike Yarwood £2.95
- ☐ ROYAL HAUNTINGS Joan Forman £3.50
- ☐ A GRAIN OF TRUTH Jack Webster £2.95
- ☐ ANOTHER VOICE Auberon Waugh £3.95
- ☐ ARMCHAIR GOLF Ronnie Corbett £3.50
- ☐ BEDSIDE RUGBY Bill Beaumont £3.50
- ☐ SWEETS Shona Crawford Poole £3.95
- ☐ DON'T ASK THE PRICE Marcus Sieff £3.95
- ☐ SQUASH BALLS Barry Waters £3.50
- ☐ BACK TO CAPE HORN Rosie Swale £3.95
- ☐ BY SEA AND LAND Robin Neillands £3.95

You can buy Fontana paperbacks at your local bookshop or newsagent. Or you can order them from Fontana Paperbacks, Cash Sales Department, Box 29, Douglas, Isle of Man. Please send a cheque, postal or money order (not currency) worth the purchase price plus 22p per book for postage (maximum postage required is £3).

NAME (Block letters) _____

ADDRESS _____

_____

_____